HATCHING YOUR MILLION
DOLLAR BUSINESS

Hatching Your Million Dollar Business
by Dan Tepke

ISBN 978-0-9883471-7-5

Photographs in the storyboards
are licensed from istockphoto.com

Net worlding PUBLISHING
Books and more that make the world better!

HATCHING YOUR MILLION DOLLAR BUSINESS

Dan Tepke

Contents

About this book

I enjoy books that provide me with the appropriate tools to accomplish specific tasks. Over time, I have collected a set of tools for a number of different tasks. I've also developed many of my own tools – like effective ways to develop actionable ideas. Simply put, although I have always found other people's books helpful, writing my own book has never been an aspiration of mine.

So, what prompted me to write this book? My catalyst was a chance introduction to author and speaker Melissa Giovagnoli Wilson. This introduction came from a mutual friend – Claudia Freed, President of Educational Assistance, Ltd. Freed serves on a variety of nonprofits boards. During our conversation, Wilson mentioned the concept of creating an idea lab on Michigan Avenue in Chicago, a place where people could visit and have their very own experiential idea creation sessions. This conversation planted the seed for writing my own book in my mind. When I mentioned to Wilson my hesitation about writing a book, she told me about the resources she makes available when she helps people write their books.

I realized I had both the tools and the coaching experience to add value to someone else's process as the person develops his/her business idea. The need was there. That was evident when I spoke to people who came to me with ideas that were either incomplete or not well thought through. If they had the right tools and processes, would that help them develop a solid idea? I looked for available books or manuals to effectively try to walk someone through this exercise – materials that use a structured process, ask questions, and provide examples and practice opportunities. After some investigation, I decided that, indeed, an opportunity was available to add some value within this particular niche. Wilson encouraged me. Once I attended one of her writing workshops, the process of working together was off and running.

Who will benefit from this book?

This book is meant for individuals who work alone or either with a few or many others. My intention is to help those inexperienced in business idea development with a simple plan for developing their own business dreams.

Anyone interested in more information on my background can refer to the section at the end of this book. For now, let me begin to help you develop a solid idea for your business.

The Basic Egg

"It's important to keep in mind that all birds, except the cuckoo bird, build their nest before laying and hatching their eggs."
~ ANONYMOUS

There's nothing easy about conceptualizing the details of your new business. We sympathize with you completely. It's easy for friends, and family to say, "Hey! You're a great cook. You should open a restaurant." But the actual concept and details of launching that restaurant are a little more complex than just having a great idea, product or service. While it may not always be easy to start a new business, it can definitely be done.

Hatching, whether it's an egg, a business, a plan or whatever simply means "to conspire to devise a plot or a plan. It's the emerging of something, whether a chicken, a fish, or an idea or a business."

That's why the "hatching your million" title for this book. I want you to consider your business idea as your golden egg, your plan, and your business concept. The key to a successful hatch is to crack that egg, or idea – just right so your business emerges ready to hit the ground running and operational. You want that rich, golden yolk of a concept to grow to the stage where it can survive outside the safe confines of the egg, or in this case, your mind. Crack open the egg too soon and you lose the potential inside because it's not strong enough to face the world. Don't care for it properly and the idea will never grow or mature, let alone hatch and take on a life of its own. Be patient and follow the plan I outline in this book if you want to succeed.

If you've ever heard the story of the Goose that laid the Golden Egg, the concept is sort of the same. In case you haven't heard it, here is a short version: A man and a woman once owned a special goose. Every day the goose would lay a golden egg, which the couple would sell. The goose made them very rich, but not rich enough. One day the wife said to the husband, "If we killed the goose we could get all the eggs at once. Then we'd really be rich." The husband agreed. So they killed the goose and cut her open only to find that she was like every other goose and there were no eggs inside her. Their haste and greed had cost them a lifetime of golden eggs.

The moral of the story is: You can't rush riches, or the development of golden eggs or business plans.

For those of you who aren't farmers, biologists or who haven't raised chickens, let's add a bit more detail and specificity:

1. You have an idea for a business. That idea came about for any of a thousand reasons. Yesterday it may have been a news story, something a friend said, or something you saw on television or in a movie. But now the thing you love has been fertilized by coming in contact with that idea.

2. Now you have the seed of a new business in your mind. It's too weak and malformed enough to really share with anyone, or to quit your job over, but you know it's got potential. You feel excited, elation, fear, hope and a desire to share your idea, to see what friends and family think. You may want to crack that idea open right then and there and share it with everyone you know,

hoping to nurture it and grow it simply by sharing it. Bad idea. What you want to do is incubate it, keep it warm and make sure it grows.

3. Protect your idea. Develop it. Prepare for the day it's ready to hatch and enter the world. That's where this book comes in. I'll show you how to nurture that egg, that plan, that idea, that potential and grow it to where it's ready to enter the world fully formed and ready to grow into a golden goose, or chicken, of your own.

You are now standing at the first step of the innovation and business process. From here on out in the beginning of each chapter the innovation flow chart will indicate your location in the innovation process. With each chapter you'll learn more and more about how to move from concept to conception to a true business. The illustration, on the next page, shows you the next steps you'll be taking.

Believe it or not, the business concept doesn't begin with the idea you have for your business. The road to being a successful entrepreneur or business owner begins with self-understanding, not with a business plan. That comes next. Until you understand yourself, your strengths, weaknesses, management style, skill sets, and so on, you can't really decide where to take your future business, or how to run it effectively. I know you're anxious to jump right in and start planning your business, but take time to do some self-assessment first.

To reach the level of self-understanding you need for this first step in starting your business, you need to begin by asking yourself some personal questions – a lot of personal questions. Once you've asked the questions, you need to answer them, then go back and review them, study them and make changes or decisions based on what you learn. They are the foundation for everything else you're going to do, so make it a solid foundation or the rest of your plan could crumble.

Innovation process flow

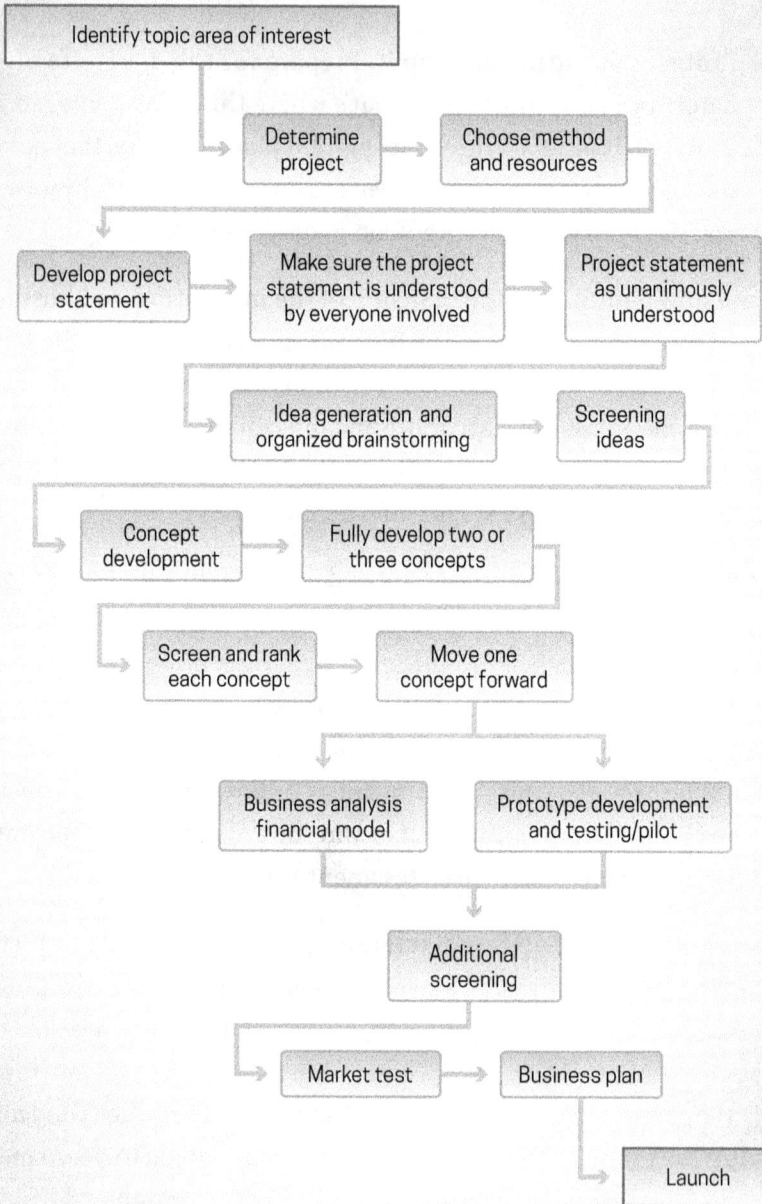

Identify topic area of interest

Determine project → Choose method and resources

Develop project statement → Make sure the project statement is understood by everyone involved → Project statement as unanimously understood

Idea generation and organized brainstorming → Screening ideas

Concept development → Fully develop two or three concepts

Screen and rank each concept → Move one concept forward

Business analysis financial model   Prototype development and testing/pilot

Additional screening

Market test → Business plan

Launch

By reviewing both questions and your answers, you'll begin to scratch the surface of who you are, and how this business is going to develop. Begin to keep a notebook or journal with the questions and answers. For right now however just review these questions to familiarize yourself with them. At the end of this chapter, you will be more prepared to answer these questions in writing. Consider these questions, which are in no particular order:

- Who are the different actors inside of you? What parts of you play an important role in your life? I.e. (parent, spouse, partner, micromanager, workaholic, party animal, nature lover, etc.)

- How focused are you?

- How flexible are you?

- How consistent are you?

- How disciplined are you?

- How do you learn?

- What challenges will you face?

- What are your strengths?

- What are your values?

- What are your passions?

- What is your ultimate goal?

- Are you a creative thinker?

- Are you a logical, managerial thinker?

- What are you **really** good at doing?

- What would you prefer **not** do? What skills and tasks will this idea require? What else will this new venture require of you (for example: money, time commitment, energy, etc.)?

- How well do you work with different types of people in different roles or functions (for example, as employees, peers, contractors or partners)?

- What energizes you?

- What intrigues you about having your own million-dollar business?

- When you daydream about this business, what do you visualize?

- What resources are available to you? (For example, friends, the Internet, professionals, family members, state/federal/local resources and centers, and other outlets.)

- Can you live an entrepreneurial life?

- As a business owner, who are you?

- What is your role in this business?

- What areas do you want to investigate?

- How do you respond to failure? Do you give up easily, or get back up and move forward?

- How are your personal and professional boundaries? Can you say "no" easily to ideas, requests and demands of others?

- Are you a people pleaser? Do you worry more about making people happy than doing the hard thing?

- Are you thin skinned? Do you react negatively to criticism, taking things personally?

- Can you accept feedback and honest critiques without getting angry? Can you make wise decisions and even change your mind if someone has a legitimate point?

- Can you ignore trolls and naysayers?

- Are you impatient, or patient with yourself and others?

- Do you have a good support group or foundation, either friends or family who strongly believe in you, or a professional organization or friend who can help you through rough times emotionally and mentally?

- Are you starting this business because you want to, or because someone else suggested it?

- Are you willing to wait three, five, and ten years or even longer to see your idea succeed? Or are you expecting success immediately?

- Are you a life long learner, willing to read, go back to school, get tutored or mentored to learn what you need to learn?

- Are you a "people person" (extrovert) or more introverted?

- Are you good at networking?

- Are you a giver or a taker?

- Do you want to make the world a better place, or simply make your world a better place?

- What motivates you? Money? Fame? Travel? Freedom? Family? Your faith? Love? Admiration from others? Being in the spotlight?

- Do you care about people, or are you simply interested in making money?

- Which appeals more to you, meeting and talking to people about your business, the social aspect of business, or the actual hands on work, research or nuts and bolts operation?

- Where do you see yourself in a year? Two years? Three? Where do you see yourself in five years, ten years? Be specific. Where do you live? What is your family situation? Do you have children? Are you traveling? Are you speaking? Famous? Happy?

- What makes you happy? Family? Work? Partying? People? Travel? Time alone or time with others? Competing, winning?

Like I said, these are hard questions. Be honest. Knowing what motivates you and what is important to you is what will keep you going when you want to give up. Knowing what you need to be happy, to remain connected, and knowing where you're going (goals) is what you'll have to have to keep moving forward. When faced with difficult decisions, knowing what your ultimate goals are is how you'll know how to make those tough decisions. You may not be able to answer all these questions right now, but you should spend time every day thinking about them. You are going into business with your most important partner – yourself. It only makes sense to know and understand whom you're going to be doing business with, right?

Nothing about developing your own business is easy, but some parts will evolve more easily than others. Only you can identify the easy (to you) parts. The difficult parts will depend on who you are and how much you understand yourself, including your skill set and knowledge. There are many ways to gain this understanding. You can read a lot of business and self-help books. You can find a good business coach or mentor. You can self-observe and get feedback from friends and family or co-workers. In addition to self-observation and using the questions sprinkled throughout this book, two other valuable resources you can

turn to are the Kolbe A™ Index and the Myers-Briggs Type Indicator®
(MBTI). You will find information about these within the chapters
that follow.

Before we examine these two tools, you need to consider your weaknesses and strengths. You may think you first need to work on your
weaknesses to make improvements, but weaknesses are not where any
million-dollar business begins. Success in any endeavor always begins
in your strengths. However, you may find that finding and applying your
strengths is trickier than it sounds.

Working from your strengths

In his book, *Management Challenges for the 21st Century*, renowned management consultant Peter Drucker dedicates a full chapter (Chapter
6) to managing oneself. The chapter opens with these questions: *What
are my strengths? What is my contribution? What are my relationships
and responsibilities?*

Drucker focuses on working from strengths because operating from our
strengths is how we succeed. However, your strengths may sometimes
deceive you. Why? Because your strengths come so naturally and easily,
you often take them for granted, devalue or overlook them. If it is that
easy to do something, you tell yourself, there must not be much value
in it – except, of course, for the person who does not have this particular strength and finds the task at hand very difficult to accomplish
without it.

Weaknesses, on the other hand, include skills that do not seem natural
to you and are difficult to improve. A funny thing happens when you
have to work hard at improving on a weakness. The more you focus on
the weakness and try to convert it to a strength, the more you begin to

place too much value on that weakness. You tend to believe you have already converted that weakness into strength. At the end of the day, focusing on that weakness just holds you back and saps your energy. Do not waste your time on weaknesses since they do not serve as a solid foundation for outstanding performance. Instead, learn, recognize and understand your strengths, then work from them. After that, find individuals who balance out your weaknesses and support your strengths. If you're bad with managing people, or money, hire those who excel in those areas. If you're an excellent engineer, but dread social situations, seek out a partner or collaborator who is strong in networking and social skills. This is where knowing your strengths is so important. You want to create a balanced team.

If you're still struggling with that concept, think of a football team, or any team sport. Everyone on the team is an athlete. That is their base strength. However, each player has different strengths, and different skill sets that make them the best person for the position they play.

The best quarterback, or first baseman, or outfielder or kicker doesn't attempt to play any position except those they're best at. They "play their position." You rarely see a linebacker sprinting out to catch a pass, although they may have to in an emergency. Their strength is in their size and the skills needed to do a specific job for the team, which is blocking the other team from reaching the quarterback.

In baseball the first baseman may sometimes be called in to help or cover the pitcher's mound in an emergency, but their strength is in being tall, flexible, fast and usually left-handed. Everyone on a team plays to their strength because that makes a stronger team. It's not that they aren't called on to use their weaker skills, but they focus on their strengths. You don't see outfielders trying to learn to throw a curve ball. They may know how, but they play to their strengths, which is the long, accurate throw to a base or cut-off man.

In individual sports, the same is true. Long distance runners don't try to become sprinters, and sprinters don't work on perfecting their marathon skills. Yes, both are runners. Yes, both can run both distances. Their strength however, is in the skill set (sprints or distance) they possess.

Doctors are the same way. There are general practitioners, and surgeons. Many general practitioners can do routine surgeries, but their strengths are in general practice. Surgeons tend to be very, very good in their specialty – orthopedic, obstetrics etc., and not so good in general medicine. They aren't necessarily bad in other areas; they're just not their strongest skill set.

Some fields, like engineering, require strong organizational, math and detail oriented skill sets, yet engineers are often noted for weak social and people skills. It's not bad to be weak in one area, or to try to improve, but focus on your strengths, the things that come easily for you, and hard for others. There are a variety of ways to do this – professional business coaches, therapy, how-to-books, seminars and personality testing. Millions of people have done this on their own and millions of others have sought professional assessments in order to move forward faster. It's up to you to decide how you want to proceed, but I highly encourage beginning with a personality test because they are very accurate in their assessments of people's strengths and weaknesses.

Utilizing the Kolbe A™ Index

The Kolbe A™ Index and the Myers-Briggs Type Indicator help determine how these tools can effectively help you create this million-dollar business.

People are different in fundamental ways. To achieve the business you envision, you'll need to surround yourself with the right mix of people as advisors, employees and peers. Just as any team needs a variety of players with different skill sets, your business will need variety as well. The people you surround yourself with should have a variety of personality profiles, instinctual styles, interests and values that complement yours, but not that necessarily match yours.

Are you a technician? A manager? An entrepreneur with a passion for business? Many new businesses start out because of a great product, idea or gadget, but fail because the business owner is not a business man or woman. They may be a great chef, inventor, artist, musician, or whatever, but they're not a businessperson. Knowing this upfront helps you design your business.

Since determining a good fit is a multi-dimensional exercise, begin by examining the role played by instincts and feelings, also called "temperament play." To best understand instinctual style, use the Kolbe A™ Index (www.Kolbe.com). This tool provides an insight into the actions, reactions and interactions, which allow individuals and groups to thrive and shape their own destinies.

The mind is multi-dimensional, with three dimensions at its foundation. These dimensions are thoughts, feelings and instincts. Knowing your instinctual style – or, in Kolbe terms, your *modus operandi*, or **MO** – enables you to make better decisions. Kolbe's instinctual styles include the **fact finder**, the **follow-through**, the **quick start** and the **implementer**.

What you learn about your personal instinctual style will help reduce conflicts, improve communications, expand effectiveness, enhance personal awareness and increase healthy behaviors. Understanding personal style, therefore, enables you to focus on your strengths. While no one's MO is better than the MO of anyone else, knowing **your** dominant style will help you better understand why you do what you do, as well as help you find people with complementary MOs. This concept supports the notion of the *power of two*, which will be discussed later.

Adding the Myers-Briggs Personality Type Indicator (MBTI)

Knowing the makeup of those around is important, however, you must also understand your own psychological, or affective, makeup. The MBTI is an excellent tool for this. Myers-Briggs offers a look into sixteen different personality types. These combinations include the **thinker or feeler**, the **sensor or intuitor**, the **judger or perceiver**, the **extravert or introvert**.

First, understand your MBTI type. There are four main dichotomies that form your type:

- introversion/introspection

- intuition/sensing

- thinking/feeling

- judging/perception

Each of these four pairs contains opposite characteristics. Your personality type consists of one from each of the four pairs. For example, you might be considered an "INFP," which means your personality traits are introversion, intuition, feeling and perception.

I suggest you take the Myers-Briggs Personality Test (http://www. personalitypathways.com/type_inventory.html) after you complete this chapter. Once you learn and understand your specific personality type, you then can seek those with complementary styles in order to attain your long-range success. A good source of information about the MBTI is the book, *Please Understand Me*, by David Keirsey and Marilyn Bates.

The Power of Two

Once you have gained the necessary insights into how you function as an individual, we then can explore the "power of two." Without an understanding of who you are, and what you bring to a partnership or collaboration, and more importantly what you don't or can't bring, you cannot successfully collaborate. Collaboration is not just two people working on different things with different skills. True collaboration is something that happens when two people truly complement each other's skill set. The two of them become more powerful when working together than when working apart.

Successful business people have three skill sets: technician, manager and entrepreneur. Typically one (or more) skill sets are your strongest. For instance, you may be a technician. You have a specific skill set and you're good at it. Maybe you can cut hair, fix and operate complex machinery, cook, write computer code, take photographs or make things with your hands. You may be an excellent real estate agent, investigator, or writer. You're very good at the thing you do that you want to turn into a business. Or, you may be a good manager, able to turn chaos into order, manage your time and money, and that of others, well. Managers have good decision making skills and are able to track the different aspects of a business, project or plan. They see the big picture and understand the small pieces that must come together to make it happen. Finally, your strength may be that of an entrepreneur, able to spot opportunities, see the big picture, attract talent, sell ideas and concepts as well as product and services. You're a risk taker and highly self-motivated. Ideally you'll have all of these skills to some degree, but people rarely do. Almost all of us excel in one area, with various competence in the others. That's where the "power of two" is so important. Collaboration in business is everything. What is collaboration? It's more than just working with someone else. It's working with someone else whose chemistry (skill sets) makes the combination of the two of you more powerful than either of you acting alone.

One of the common examples of how collaboration is more powerful is oxygen and acetylene, the two gases that combine to create the white-hot flame of a welder's blowtorch. Separately both oxygen and acetylene will burn, but together they create a fire hot enough to melt metal. That's how they complement each other – by creating something more explosive and vital together than alone.

Rodd Wagner and Gayle Muller write about the power of collaboration and use the example of oxygen and acetylene in their book, "The Power of 2: How to Make the Most of Your Partnerships at Work and in Life [Gallup Press 2009]. After much research and study what they found was that the best collaborations share three things:

- The collaborators complement each other's strengths

- The collaborators need each other to get the job done

- Each partner believes strongly that the other does some things better than they do, and that they do some things better than their partner.

All three of those qualities, the authors noted, must be present for any collaboration to be successful.

At the beginning of this chapter, you were asked to reflect on questions about the skills you have and the skills you need. As a general rule, it takes two people with complementary skills and abilities to accomplish a truly successful business. Countless examples of this rule in action exist.

Consider billionaire investor Warren Buffett. A large portion of the financial world views his annual letter to stockholders as a source of knowledge and inspiration. In Buffett's letter reviewing the 2009 Berkshire Hathaway performance, Buffet writes a little about some of Berkshire Hathaway's holdings as well as about the leadership of a number of companies. Buffett himself is the one who gets the most media attention; however, few realize that Buffet has an equally gifted and skilled partner, Charlie Munger. Munger has worked with Buffet for years. The public may not see it, but Munger provides the company with a skill set that complements Buffet's. Buffet himself admits his unbridled enthusiasm for so many things is well tempered by Munger's skepticism. They need each other to achieve the balance that makes them both successful. Buffet has dubbed Munger "the Abominable 'No' Man" and admits that together they make better investment decisions than he could ever make alone.

You may want to do an Internet search for a talk given by Charles Munger at the USC Business School in 1994, called "A Lesson On Elementary, Worldly Wisdom as it Relates to Investment Management and Business," to see if you can pick up some clues. If you read through Buffett's 2009 annual letter, you'll realize he also tends to identify two key people at each of his firms. Is it possible that each of these individuals brings complementary skill sets to their individual firms? I'd say probably.

Intel is another example of a company where two individuals with complementary skills share one role. This organizational structure is known as "two-in-the-box." The two-in-the box format is used to stabilize a transition or a start-up company by adding skills and knowledge that broaden the job capacity. For example, an operations-oriented person is best paired with a marketing-focused one. While I'm talking about this, it's important to realize something else:

Don't confuse collaboration with friendship. They aren't mutually exclusive, but they are often mistaken for collaboration when they're not. Getting along with your collaborator is important, but complimenting each other's skill sets, personality and strengths is more important than liking each other.

To assess who might be your best partner, first consider what role you plan to play in the business. Remember: play from your strengths. If your strength is in marketing, lead from the marketing perspective, but find individuals to fill in for your weaknesses in other areas. In the beginning, this may be a trusted friend simply because they are the person you have access to at the time. However, as cash flow improves, the role may be outsourced and later converted to a full-time position within the company. If your skills are in organization and process, lead from that point of view and find others to handle the marketing, or not.

Consider who would make the best business partner, not the best business friend, for you. Whose skill sets complement yours? Surprisingly enough, many people naturally fall into a complementary relationship as friends, particularly from a young age. Others of us must seek out and find a complementary partner from our social network, work, or through our field of interest.

Friendships and family members can be excellent partners and complement us well, but they are not always the best collaboration choice. On the other hand, many siblings, friends and family members have formed famous collaborations: Orville and Wilbur Wright, brothers Richard and Maurice McDonald and Ray Kroc (McDonald's hamburger chain), Bill Gates and Paul Allen (childhood friends), Steve Jobs and Steve Wozinak (childhood friends), Ben Cohen and Jerry Greenfield of Ben & Jerry's Ice Cream (childhood friends). The important thing is to find someone whose skills and strengths compliment yours and vice versa. Know what each of you brings to the collaboration, and cannot bring. This is not a time to forgo collaboration in place of being friends. You get the picture.

The journey begins

You, in all likelihood, have little to no dough and have been thinking about creating your own business for some time. Since you purchased this book, I imagine you also are now becoming serious about moving ahead with and acting on your thinking. You've read the questions, now know that somewhere along the line you're going to need a collaborator or partner (full or part-time), and you're thinking about who you are, and what your strengths are, and where your weaknesses lie.

It sounds like a lot of touchy-feely introspection right? Depending on your personality style that's either a good thing, or an annoying one. Either way, it is necessary. An understanding and awareness of your internal mental and psychological processes will greatly assist you as you move forward. Emotional self-awareness is also important. You must understand and connect with what is going on internally with what you are thinking and feeling if you're going to be in control of your decisions and actions.

Whatever your feelings and thoughts are is tremendously important, and also natural. Fear, apprehension, excitement, doubts, confidence, are all normal feelings for any entrepreneur no matter what their personality type. Some will be more fearful, others less. Be aware that almost everyone on a similar journey experiences the same feelings and emotions in some degree. To understand the internal processes and to be conscious of those processes as you travel along your journey will make it more understandable, and thus more tolerable, but not necessarily more comfortable. Every individual and team goes through these initial feelings of doubt, excitement, fear, anticipation, frustration, anger, joy and elation. While everyone's experience is unique, each step of the internal process I'll describe in this book will be present at some point during the duration of your project.

Two parallel processes take place as you begin your journey – the how-to process, and the emotional/mental/spiritual process. The obvious and practical process is to follow these steps to develop your idea into a successful business concept. Refer back to the innovation flow chart at the beginning of each chapter to chart your progress. These steps will be explained in depth as you continue to read this book.

The other process involves your internal experience. You'll need to be aware of and work through those stages as well if you want to succeed. The next section will identify stages of the journey and relate them to the internal experience.

Each stage of the internal process has three basic components: emotions, cognition and actions.

- *Emotions* are all about feelings.

- *Cognition* is the process of knowing, perceiving and remembering.

- *Action* is driven by the need to get something done and is the doing.

Based on observations of both individuals and teams over the years, here are the stages of this process: **pre-decision, exploration, introduction, launch** and **autonomy.** Each stage features different emotions as well as cognitive activities and actions.

Emotions play an important role in influencing you into action or inaction. These emotions vary from anger to desire to fear or joy, excitement and even elation. It's not the emotion itself that determines success or failure. People can be terrified, but act anyway and succeed.

Helen Gurley Brown, the famous editor of Cosmopolitan Magazine in the mid-60s, tells people that after her first day on the job, knowing nothing about running a magazine, she curled up in a fetal position under her desk and cried. But she went back to work the next day and the next. She was terrified, but didn't let her fear stop her. She literally retreated to the space under her desk when she needed to, but she understood that her internal process didn't have to control her external actions.

You'll find that some emotions, even positive ones, can lead to inaction and failure. These emotions include elation, joy and happiness. Entrepreneurs, especially those who are initially very successful at sales, or funding their business, or who have an early advantage, can get caught up in the excitement, romance, fame, fortune and attention and neglect the grunt work – the hard work that sustains a business. You're so busy celebrating success you forget that it's not locked in, that it must be nurtured, fed and maintained. Sometime the positive emotions can be the most destructive ones because they lull us into a sense of security and laziness. Positive emotions can also motivate us, if we're aware of their power.

Some examples of emotions that move you to action: anger, desire fear, passion, euphoria, and self-confidence. Emotions that lead to inaction are anxiety, dread, worry, apathy, despair disappointment, contentment, relaxed, calmness, indifference happiness.

Positive or negative, everyone must find the emotion(s) that stops them, and the emotion that moves them when inaction takes over. The fear of failing your family, or the fear of going bankrupt may be a more powerful and motivating fear than the fear of looking foolish or silly. Over time you'll discover what paralyzes you as well as moves you through fear. This is part of understanding yourself and your personality style and strengths. These motivators can change over time, so beware of that as well.

Cognition is mental processing that builds your knowledge base. Cognition can occur through processes such as calculating, reasoning, and concept formulation. Problem solving, decision-making, memory, pattern recognition and mental imagery are other examples of cognitive processes.

Actions - An action is the component that materializes an idea. It's what truly "hatches" your million dollar business. Actions are typically physical, but they always begin with a mental and emotional decision to act and to move in a direction. Action is all about doing. Below is a closer examination of each stage.

Stage one: Pre-decision

Emotions - Whenever you have a variety of decisions to make your emotions may be scattered. They can range from nervousness and stress to excitement and fear, or a combination of fear and excitement. Even veteran performers, athletes, speakers and politicians admit that after decades of doing what they do they still get nervous before they act, speak, play or perform. They say they would worry if they didn't – because their emotions drive them to do their best. In stage one, pre-decision, you can expect to feel nervous, excited, stressed, elated, worried, brave, fearful or hopeful. Those aren't the only emotions you may experience, but they're the most common.

Cognitive - Keeping the right mindset is essential while creating the fundamentals of your company. You may or may not be buffeted by doubts. You may feel confident and positive. Either way, emotions are like the weather in the south, hang around long enough and everything changes. Your emotions will change hour-to-hour, day-to-day and week-to-week no matter what you're doing or what is happening with your business. That's normal.

What matters is that your cognitive processes during this period includes reasoning, problem solving, and decision making independent of your feelings. Remember Helen Gurley Brown? Crawl under your desk and cry, go for a run, punch a pillow, play a video game, or whatever healthy, non-addictive thing you have to do to cope with the emotions. Just don't let them control your actions, reasoning and decisions.

Pay attention to your intuition, but learn to distinguish it from fear or doubt, confidence and elation. Intuition is not an emotion; it's a knowing based on your subconscious.

Actions - Make sure that your actions during this stage are calculating, organized and based on data, facts and research. Try recording your thinking, collecting data, and assessing probabilities.

Many of your actions are going to be routine and structured, but many won't be. Life and business aren't always black and white. The right decision is not always the easy one, and the easy decision is not always the right one.

I'm sure at some point you have seen a cartoon of a person with an angel on one shoulder. On the other shoulder is a devil, complete with pitchfork. Both are whispering directly contradictory statements in each ear. The challenge obviously, is to decide which voice you should listen to. Sometimes the struggle is going to be a moral and ethical one. Sometimes you're going to have to choose between the lesser of two horrible options. You may even have the enviable struggle of which of two or more opportunities is the better path.

When you find yourself struggling to make a decision one way or the other, you'll not only begin to doubt yourself, you'll also find yourself debating with the voices . You'll realize you're playing both sides, asking which voices (thoughts) to listen to. You'll (hopefully) weigh the consequences and risks. You'll ask, "What's the truth here?" or "What is your mind/fear over-amplifying or exaggerating? What's a fear and what's merely imagination? Where is your attention? What is realistic and what is magical or hopeful thinking?

If this internal debate becomes too intense, rendering you unable to make a strong decision, then it's time to stop the debate. Examine each debated point or argument you're replaying in your head. Get out a pad of paper and write down each point of every argument and collect data about each. Work on each of these points until you are confident you have determined a solution or a resolution for each. Does your data point move you ahead or show you that delaying moving your idea forward is better? Sometimes staying in your current situation feels safe, but often this current situation will feel empty. Whether or not you move your new business idea ahead is entirely your choice, but it should be based on a thorough examination of all sides. You may want to write everything down, and then set it aside for a day or two and come back to it. Take time to get away from the issue and clear your head. Work on something else. Take a break, and then return when you feel refreshed. Sometimes a good meal and a good night's sleep is all it takes to see things in a better, clearer light.

Stage two Exploration

- **Emotions** - During stage two you're going to feel excited, zeal, surprise, wonder, hope, fear, desire fear and stress. They're normal feelings. Expect them to come and go, mix and mingle, and even go completely away at times, leaving you feeling numb. Don't worry. They'll return.

- **Cognition** - Your emotions may take center stage, but don't forget to pay attention to your logical, cognitive process as well. Cognition is the **pattern** recognition, perception, calculating, concept formulation and decision-making elements involved in stage two.

- **Actions** - Hopefully you'll use your emotions and your cognition to gather information, record, develop, diagram possibilities, gather evidence and explore your risk assessment during stage two. Actions are where you gather all the data, information, intuition and risks and leap, or stride confidently forward, putting your decisions into play.

Action is also the stage of "Preparing to leap." This preparation will also bring your individual characteristics into play. It's important at this stage not to compare yourself with anyone. Each person prepares to make, and actually makes the leap into a new adventure differently.

Some individuals can make the jump without much investigation or accumulating much data, while others may need to be well prepared. There are analytical personality types that have to have an in-depth investigation with more data than would ever be needed by most. They feel a need to conduct a full analysis, as well as develop a highly detailed plan regarding how to move ahead and all the potential consequences of their decision before they'll even consider taking that first step.

Others will consider an idea briefly, think it sounds wonderful and make the leap with no more than a cursory (if that) glance at the data. They operate on their gut feelings and confidence in their ability to spot an opportunity when they see it.

Sometimes after an exploratory investigation, or tentative step into a decision an individual will change their minds. They will decide not to move forward. Their reasons may include their current obligations, lack of confidence, risk aversion, lack of supporting data or just plain fear. At other times, after only a preliminary investigation, an individual is more than ready to take the next step. The most important point to keep in mind is that once the decision is made, it must be a conscious decision on the individual's part. Moving forward because a partner, spouse, friend or your family thinks it's best when you're not so convinced it is, is important. To stick with a decision and successfully see it through, it must be your own. Good or right decisions don't ensure smooth sailing. They just cast you out into the sea so you can make your way.

Oddly enough, once you make the commitment to move ahead, interesting things begin to happen that will impact your project. Helpful information and the right people and resources will appear or will be discovered. For example, an advisor may materialize through your research and will help you through the process. As you move forward, you will leave what you know behind. You'll enter a world in which no matter how good your research, data gathering and analysis are, you will encounter unknown rules, situations, boundaries and challenges. This leads to the final stage of exploration. Remember, exploration is supposed to be fun, challenging and a bit scary.

Back in the day when there was a lot of world to be discovered mapmakers drew maps of all they knew of the existing world, and then in the blank, unexplored regions they wrote a warning to travelers and explorers: "Beyond here there be dragons." I don't know if that was supposed to warn explorers off, or encourage them, but it certainly reflected the way most of us feel when venturing into uncharted ventures.

You may begin to have "second thoughts," have "buyer's remorse," or begin to think, "why did I decide to do this?" You may see dragons where none exist. During this phase, you move from the known to the unknown. This can be the point where your greatest fear exists. You may find the angel on one shoulder and the devil on the other are both yelling at you at the top of their lungs. This is the jump-off spot where you'll enter a new stage of your journey. This is the point at which you must be willing to leave the old behind.

In the 1999 hit movie, The Matrix, Morpheus, the leader of a small group of reality seekers, offers Neo, the movie's protagonist, a blue pill or a red pill. He then says:

"This is your last chance. After this, there is no turning back. You take the blue pill, the story ends. You wake up in your bed and believe whatever you want to believe. You take the red pill, you stay in Wonderland and I show you how deep the rabbit-hole goes."

Neo of course takes the red pill and his life is never the same. You will be confronted with a similar choice at some point. Do you want to see what can happen if you commit and act and hatch your business? Or do you want to retreat and pretend you never could have made it anyway? The choice is always yours to make.

Stage three: Introduction

For those of you who have wrestled dragons, debated critics, searched your soul, made up your mind and decided to "take the red pill," to see a different future, you'll begin to move ahead. What can you expect on this journey? Not only will a full range of emotions appear during stage three, but the level of the intensity of these emotions will also begin to rise. Exhilaration, joy and excitement will accompany an adrenaline rush, which dominates your feelings. This is normal for any new venture. We experienced it as children on the first day of school. We experienced as teens or adults when we started our first job, or went into the military, or accepted a new responsibility. New beginnings are wonderful, exciting and emotional at any age. Welcome to stage three.

The introduction phase consists of the **tests and hurdles, completeness, temptations, conformation, home stretch** and the **goal.**

If you have not already experienced this as an entrepreneur, once the excitement and newness of your office, your plan, your business wears off you'll discover a path filled with tasks, tests and challenges that take the place of the shininess of the new life you've chosen. Over the course of these challenges and tests, you will find that each task and test requires your immediate attention and effort as it appears. Each task or test must be completed successfully. This means you must persist until you succeed. Expect to fail. Expect to get up and try again. Expect to repeat this exercise thousands of times over your life. It's normal. You never truly fail until you fail to get up and try again.

The journey you have embarked on is not for the meek or mild; it is suited only for the courageous. If you get knocked down, get back up. Just as a child learning to walk, or a skier learning to ski, most entrepreneurs rarely succeed on their first try. You didn't learn to walk the first time you tried. We learn by failing. It's not personality defect, it's a necessary part of success. The man or woman who says they've never failed has never succeeded.

You will fail, succeed and even barely make it at times. Your emotions will change as rapidly as a ride on a world-class roller coaster. You'll edge slowly up steep peaks. Those long slow climbs to the high peaks will last much, much longer than the exhilaration you find at the brief seconds at the apex. Your moment on the top of the mountain will always be followed quickly by a fast descent into a deep trough, usually punctuated by your terrified screams as you descend. On the way down you may be afraid you'll never again see a mountaintop. Don't worry. You will, at least as long as you get up and try again.

You must be flexible and work hard, but you also must work smart. Remember, this is a time to transform from the old to the new on many levels. This type of change takes place only through significant effort and dedication. Enjoy the ride. That's part of the process.

As you progress in creating your business, you will gradually become the business. You will develop a blind love for this endeavor and a passion for its success. You will feel certain **completeness.** For entrepreneurs, their business becomes part of them; it becomes their child. You may believe nothing could distract you from your pursuit. But you'd be wrong. Temptation and distraction abound when you're an entrepreneur.

What might cause you to stray off this road where you are creating something new? **Although temptations** may divert you in directions leading away from the goal you have chosen, they won't always be obvious temptations. Sometimes you'll be distracted by other opportunities and bargains. Sometimes you'll think that adding more, changing horses in mid-stream, or altering your vision to incorporate someone else's vision or business is a good thing. But there's a good chance it's a distraction, a temptation or an unexamined decision or non-relevant opportunity that can take your business down.

You must remain conscious of your actions, your feelings, your thoughts and your goals, and most importantly *your* vision throughout this journey. Focus on what you need to do and what you hope to accomplish. Don't allow yourself to become distracted by opportunities that don't forward your movement and progress to your dream. As one expression goes, "It's hard to remember your goal was to drain the pond when you find yourself up to your eyeballs in beautiful mermaids (or alligators)."

Later in this book, you will learn how to develop a **project statement**. This project statement will serve to remind you of your goals and provide a guide by which to measure how effectively you stay focused on your efforts, as well as evaluate any opportunities that may come your way. This project statement helps you avoid sidetracks that lead nowhere. It also helps you resist the urge to take on projects and challenges that aren't related to your goals. You also may find that, as work becomes more difficult, temptations to do other things grow. Procrastination sets in. You may well find yourself engaged in activities, conferences, or tasks unrelated to your project. You may feel busy, but you're not really. You're just spinning your wheels so you don't have to move forward, or confront a new situation, or deal with something or someone unpleasant.

Be aware of the activities and decisions you undertake and how they relate to your goals. Ask yourself if those activities are related closely to your project or are these actions activities that cause you to avoid your project? When avoidance activities take place business development activities suffer. The business development journey has many guideposts. The most important one – the one that forms the center of your journey – is when you encounter someone or something so powerful that it creates a transformation in you. The old ways are gone and both you and your project now transform, becoming one entity. An example of this is a group which finds its unique niche in the market. Sometimes, this transforming moment comes as **confirmation** or acknowledgment from a known, important figure in the field. Confirmation by an expert brings life and energy to the project; additional steps begin to fall into place.

Suddenly, you find that you no longer need to run at a fever pitch. You can see and feel your progress. You are in the **home stretch**; indeed, the prize you seek is within sight. You have defied the odds and now you're able to see, feel and smell victory.

Your **goal** is achieved. Your million dollar business idea is now launched and a reality. Emotions and feelings differ at this point. For some there is a feeling of the loss of the adventure, the thrill of the chase, the adrenaline of the race and the risk. For others, the sense of relief, excitement, and exhilaration is completely rewarding. There's a sense of "I'd never do it again in a million years, but I wouldn't take a million dollars for the experience."

Stage four: Post Launch

- **Emotions** - excitement, elation, happiness, passion, renewed zeal and zest, contentment, serenity, calmness, emptiness and sadness all are typical emotions for this stage.

- **Cognition** - Decision making, calculation, reasoning and achieving solutions are among the cognitive elements found in stage four.

- **Actions** - Leading and managing things, establishing priorities, maintaining order, focusing, risk-taking, promoting, creating tangible goods

Post launch emotions can be challenging. Some people feel relief, others feel depression or anxiety. Self-doubt and fear can set in even though the launch was successful. Stay on track. Focus on your next step and your goal. The fear will diminish over time.

When you reach the **focus point** – the point where you have your fully developed product or service, or business model, and your business plan is complete and the business is operating – you have achieved your goal. You'll experience elation from your success and want it to last as long as possible. Hang onto that feeling, however, now is the time to return to "real" life. The adrenaline rush and the excitement of the hunt can become your new objective if you're not careful. Pursuing the adrenaline rush can cloud the work it takes to launch and maintain a business. Some entrepreneurs, unable to focus on running the business, inadvertently drive themselves down unrelated paths. For those individuals, disaster may soon follow.

Conversely, sometimes immediately after your goal is achieved, you may experience the feeling of a loss of **control**. Be it real or imagined, you may feel that someone or something is trying to take away what you have created. Pay attention to these fears. They may be unfounded, or they could be intuitive feelings about a real threat. This is the exact time to increase your efforts to protect your business while you work to achieve a "normal" operating environment. Ask yourself why you might be feeling what you're feeling. Get in the habit of journaling things as regularly as possible. It will help you identify where your feelings and fears are originating and help you track your creative process as well.

If you're feeling threatened, examine the possible causes. Have you ignited a competition with another firm? Is someone trying to duplicate your idea? Have others told you, or implied they thought they could create the same product or business and do a better job? Remember, in business, periods of tranquility do not last very long. Neither do periods of fear, panic or paranoia.

If you're feeling threatened or challenged, that's all the more reason to find appropriate **advisors**. They're another vital step in protecting your business. The post-launch phase is one in which you begin to seek out individuals with skill sets different from yours. Look for those people with the personalities and other key characteristics that offer important resources to your business. Don't rush, and don't grab the first person that seems to fit the bill. Take your time and make sure you're a good match. Do your due diligence and be patient when selecting employees and collaborators you haven't worked with before.

The entrepreneur's journey is long and difficult. It requires assistance and specialized advice in order to move the business from one stage to the next. Each stage requires different skill sets and different types of advice. Who are your appropriate, trusted resources for each stage? Have you looked far enough ahead to have an idea? Or will you need to hire a headhunter or recruiter? Some people have a wide range of contacts and friends to draw from; others have to diligently search to find the right person. Start looking for people before you need them so you too have a pool of prospects to choose from, and aren't forced to hire someone out of an urgent, immediate need. Also consider the people already working for you. Do they have the potential to expand their current skill sets? Can you groom them for more responsibility and other positions?

Once you find the right advisors, start thinking about, and looking for someone with whom you can collaborate. While many entrepreneurs do succeed on their own, it's rare to find a successful business owner without an equally skilled and passionate collaborator. Great partnerships don't just happen. They must be forged, fed and nurtured, just like your business.

Once you cross over from the excitement of creating your business to enter the post-launch phase, the trick will be to carry with you all the **wisdom** you've accumulated over the course of your adventure. This wisdom is essential to your business success. You also need to share this new knowledge within your company and with your new employees and your collaborator. Sharing wisdom and knowledge with employees is not always easy, even when you've hired good people. Some people just don't like change. Some may not respect authority. Others may be content not to grow and improve and will resent you for suggesting they do.

Many associates will not understand, appreciate or relate to your experiences or the knowledge you've gained. As a result, they will find it difficult to relate to the wisdom you are sharing with them. Finding a way to relate your insights to their jobs in a way they can appreciate and embrace it will always be a challenge. This is where a collaborator can come in. You may have a gift with words and people, or not. An effective communicator and collaborator could provide just the experience and expertise you need to move forward with your employees.

However you convince your employees to get on board, if you successfully communicate your accumulated wisdom to those around you, you will have become the master of two worlds. You now not only have the competence, skills and knowledge to create a business, but also to successfully operate your own ongoing business. Pat yourself on the back. You achieved these skills while overcoming many of your internal fears and achieving balance in your own life.

Step five: Autonomy

- **Emotions** - happiness, alertness, self-confidence, relaxation and tranquility are typical emotions to experience during stage five.

- **Cognition** - problem-solving, increased memory, improved reasoning and more competent calculation are examples of the cognitive activities during stage five.

- **Actions** - leadership, as well as providing history, guidance and focus now operate within established systems, procedures and a business model as typical actions during this stage.

The final step in this process is attaining freedom. *Mastery leads to a freedom from fear, or the freedom to act in spite of fear. In turn, mastery also provides independence, which provides a license to do as one wants within the bounds of the business model.* It is the great ability to live in the moment, focusing on your business, but not having to worry about the future or regret the past.

You are now familiar with the stages of this process outside of business development efforts. You also have been introduced to the possible emotions, cognitive activity and actions associated with each stage, which may come into play during your journey. As you travel your path, try to stay aware of these emotions and what impact they have on you your project. Do they move you to further action or do they stop you cold in your tracks? Being aware of how you feel and understanding your reaction to these feelings is crucial. The success of your project depends on this awareness of yourself. You'll find as you become more skilled and experienced that your awareness, your emotions and the things which motivate you may change. Doing frequent self-assessments, such as once or twice a year, can help you stay on top of these changes. Journaling or keeping a diary of events, decisions and struggles can also prove to be an excellent self-assessment tool. Depending on how detailed or specific your entries are, as you read back over the journal at the end of the year you'll actually be able to see how much you've learned, changed and grown.

Are you ready to make the leap?

Do you remember the questions posed at the beginning of this chapter? Now that you have a better understanding of why that self-awareness matters, it's time to pull out your notebook and begin to answer those questions. The questions are repeated below. Write out the answers and refer to them as you progress along your journey. Writing the answers in pen or pencil in a journal rather than typing them into a document will help your brain process and remember them better. It also personalizes the entries and helps your subconscious process them more effectively. Don't set the journal aside once you've answered the questions. This should be an evolving process throughout your business career.

Referring to your answers as a reference will help you in the evolution of your million-dollar business idea.

Questions:

Begin by describing the different actors inside of you. "Actors" refers to the different parts of yourself. You may be the CEO, an inventor, an engineer, a family man/woman, a partner, an artist, a businessman, and a salesperson. All these "parts" are what we call actors. You may respond differently to a situation as a friend, than as a businessperson. It's important to know that. Who are you? Who are the parts of you that make you who you are, or who you want to be?

Questions About You

- How focused are you?

- How flexible are you?

- How consistent are you?

- How disciplined are you?

- How do you learn?

- What challenges will you face?

- What are your strengths?

- What are your values?

- What are your passions?

- What is your ultimate goal?

- Are you a creative thinker?

- Are you a logical, managerial thinker?

- What are you **really** good at doing?

- What would you prefer **not** do?

- What skills and tasks will this idea require? What else will it require from you (for example: money, time commitment, energy, etc.)?

- How well do you work with different types of people in different roles or functions (for example, employees, peers, contractors or partners)?

- What energizes you?

- What intrigues you about having your own million-dollar business?

- When you daydream about this business, what do you visualize?

- What resources are available to you? (These include friends, Internet, professionals, family members, state/federal/local resources and centers?)

- Can you live an entrepreneurial life?

- As a business owner, who are you?

- What is your role in this business?

- What areas do you want to investigate?

Your Thinking

- How do you learn?

- Do you frame your thinking in a creative way?

- Do you frame your thinking in a more logical, liner manner?

Leadership

- What is your leadership style?

- What leadership skills and talent will be required to hatch your own business successfully?

- How will you work with different people and their styles?

- How will you try to fill the many different roles of the entrepreneur?

- What roles will you not try to fill yourself?

What Resources

- Talent?

- Funds?

- Time?

Goal/Vision

- When you daydream about hatching your own business, what do you visualize?

- What is your ultimate goal?

After you answer these questions, reread them and use them to build your personal profile. Be honest with yourself as you evaluate this profile. You're the only one who will see the answers, so be honest with yourself, even if it's painful or embarrassing to do so. No one is perfect. Few people have all the skill sets they need to succeed when they first start a business. Being a successful entrepreneur is more about how you respond to failure and hard decisions, and not so much about having every exact skill set needed to solve the problems yourself.

The entrepreneurial life is sacrificial, full of failures, and often comes with one crisis after the next. Does your profile fit that of a person who can maintain an entrepreneurial life? You will find yourself short on time, but you will experience a great sense of accomplishment as you hit the heights and attain unimaginable rewards, both material and psychological.

What is the entrepreneurial profile? Since not all entrepreneurs are the same, here are some words that describe the general entrepreneurial profile. The more traits you have, the more likely you are to succeed. If you're an entrepreneur chances are you're:

- independent, likes challenges and enjoys risk-taking,

- intense and strong-willed, as well as obsessive, competitive and intolerant,

- someone who seeks thrills and adventure,

- a person who is a visionary, but also is self-absorbed, tough and smart.

- Someone who takes what they do seriously. You recognize a business is a business, not a glorified hobby. You aren't easily distracted.

- Someone who is not easily dissuaded from a path and can bounce back quickly and more determined to succeed after a failure or rejection.

- Someone who plans, is organized, keeps lists, and tracks milestones and goals.

- Often someone with a short attention span. If you can identify a trusted friend who will provide you with realistic and honest feedback, then certainly share your profile with this friend and listen intently to this person's comments.

- Manage money wisely or have a collaborator who does.

- Aren't afraid to ask for the sale.

- Doesn't take the word no personally.

- Know your customers or clients inside out. You know whom you're selling to and why.

- A shameless self-promoter, without being obnoxious or arrogant about it.

- Charismatic and project a positive, pleasant personality and feeling on people you meet.

- Genuinely like people and want to help them and get to know them.

- Keep up with technology and aren't afraid to use it, or hire someone who can.

- A team player. You realize and appreciate the fact that no man/woman is an island and you can't do it alone. You know how to get along with people, even if you don't like them.

- Are willing to seek out information and become known as an expert in your field rather than relying on others to feed you information and advice.

- Are competitive. You're not afraid to work hard and do more to be better.

- You respect and invest in yourself, taking the training or getting the coaching and advice you need to improve yourself and your skills.

- You value reputation and credibility and strive to create it even in the face of risk, failure and competition from unscrupulous competitors.

- You understand the difference between features and benefits and sell benefits. This shows you understand the problem your customer is trying to solve.

- Are an excellent negotiator. You understand that success in business means getting both or all sides a fair and equitable deal wherever and whenever possible.

- You value family and aren't afraid to take time off to be with them.

- Pursue a win-win attitude in your interactions with others, whether they're customers or employees.

- Are skilled in the art of follow-up. You don't micro-manage, but you keep a finger on every pulse of your operation. You aren't shy about following through, getting back to people about requests and projects.

Sound daunting? Don't worry. The person who has all of these qualities and characteristics hasn't been born. These are things to strive for. That's where your journal will come in handy. Write down who you think you are, and who you want to be. Set goals and start working on them one at a time. One day you'll look up and see the more successful your business is, the closer you are to being everything on this list.

CHAPTER 2

Design your million-dollar idea

"The key to everything is patience. You get the chicken by hatching the egg, not by smashing it."
~ ARNOLD H. GLASGOW, AMERICAN AUTHOR

I know you're anxious to move on and get to the nuts and bolts of designing and perfecting your idea. However, if you have not yet completed the questions at the end of the first chapter, go back and do it. You cannot expect to move onto the next step until you complete this first one. If your composite self-profile is not complete, you will be unable to proceed smoothly. Finish it now. Your million-dollar adventure waits. The better your self-assessment, the more rock solid your foundation, and your business, will be.

Finished with your self-assessment? Good. After you have attained a deeper knowledge of yourself, you will better be able to design your breakout company. If you do not have a "big idea" already, do not worry. Many companies have evolved over time. Some begin with a big idea, and some without it.

In the well-researched book, *Built to Last*, by authors Jim Collins and Jerry Porras, the two men reveal that Hewlett Packard began when Bill Hewlett and Dave Packard founded a company, and *then* worked to discover what the company would manufacture. The idea for Texas

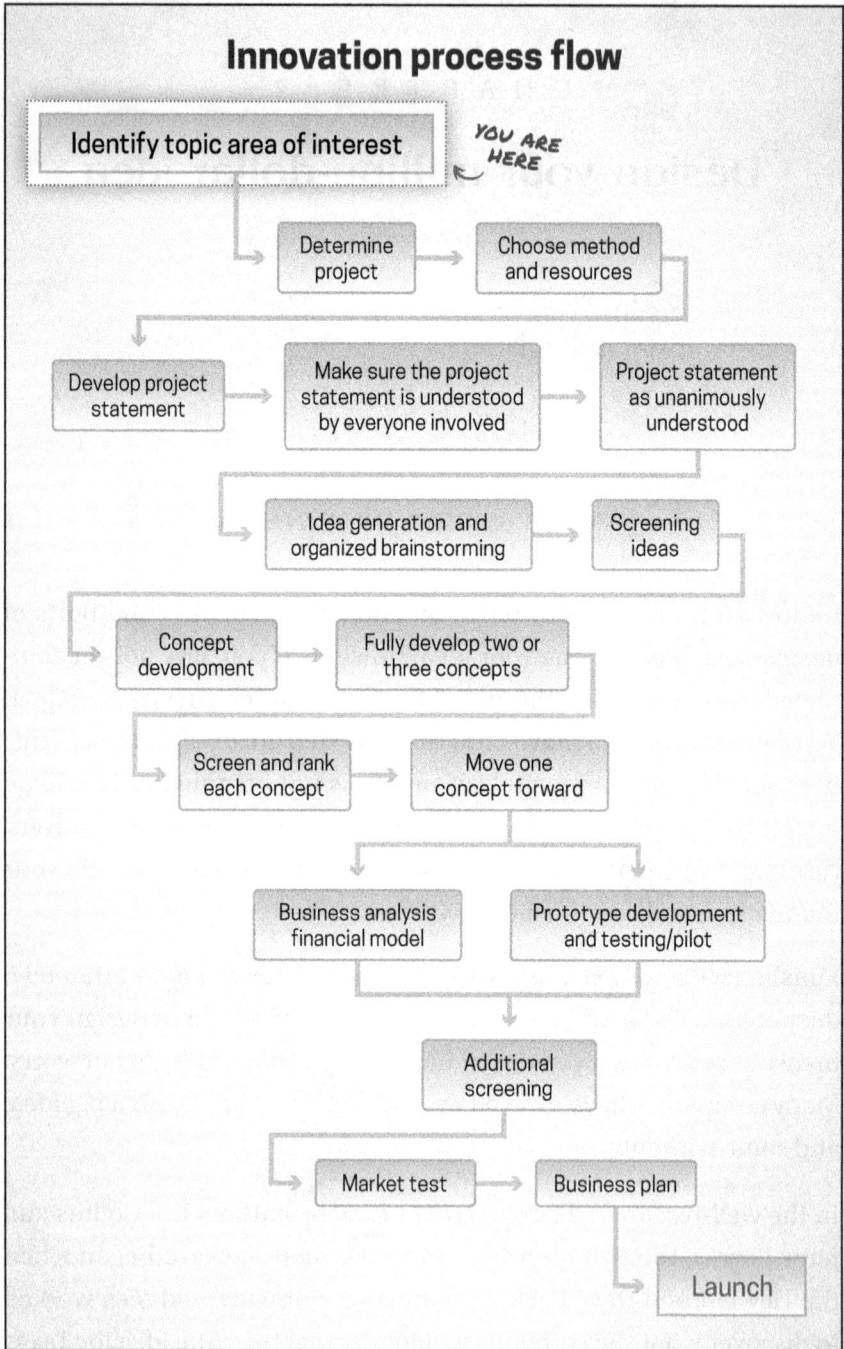

Innovation process flow

Identify topic area of interest

YOU ARE HERE

Determine project

Choose method and resources

Develop project statement

Make sure the project statement is understood by everyone involved

Project statement as unanimously understood

Idea generation and organized brainstorming

Screening ideas

Concept development

Fully develop two or three concepts

Screen and rank each concept

Move one concept forward

Business analysis financial model

Prototype development and testing/pilot

Additional screening

Market test

Business plan

Launch

Instruments Corporation (TI) evolved from a business development process with a highly defined and developed business concept. Sony, founded by Masaru Ibuka, began much like Hewlett Packard. Ibuka founded the company and then began to brainstorm about what the company would actually do. (Additional company names below have been altered to protect identities.)

In the insurance arena, "Mike H" had an idea for a company, which, over time, became a marketing consulting firm, then a Washington lobbying firm, followed by becoming an insurance company. It evolved into a software provider, morphing back toward becoming an insurance company. It now develops analytical math models.

As the work begins in earnest to launch your million-dollar business idea, you will begin to craft that idea. The key here is to craft that most important idea now, whether it changes in the future or not.

As you begin to craft your idea, it melds and synchronizes your dedication, your involvement and mastery of these idea details with your own being. If you truly know your own capabilities and have the necessary resources available at hand, the process to craft your million-dollar idea will be easier. To maintain a better grasp of this information, list your ideas in the form of a "project statement," described below. Don't rush it. Crafting this project statement takes time. The time spent crafting it will allow you to reap better results. An example of a project statement may be "Develop a game for families to play," or "Develop a business in 'human care'."

In these early development stages, it is important that you work predominately from the right side of your brain, which is more creative and less judgmental. Gradually, over time, you will move your idea toward the left side of the brain, which is much more analytical and judgmental. You need both sides to be effective.

The right side of the brain deals with metaphors, dreams, humor and ambiguity. Fantasies, paradoxes, hunches and generalizations play out here. This part of the brain is far more childlike and drawn to fun and silliness.

Activities begin with the formulation of what I call a "project statement." The project statement is a combination of right- and left-brain thinking. After you have established the project statement, your brain activity will generally move back and forth between left- and right-brain as you work on setting goals and visualizing your next steps. This may or may not evoke emotions, frustration or indecision as the two sides of your brain wrestle with your decisions. This is normal. Acknowledge the struggle and keep moving forward.

What is a "project statement?"

A "project statement" is the guide you choose to use to define your business goal. The statement should present your objective broadly in one short sentence. For example, "Develop a business in human care." Next, determine your parameters. An example of this statement would be, "Owning my own profitable business." The statement should continue by setting some guidelines. Here are some guideline examples: a product category, development costs, the time frame from development to launch, time from launch to profitability, the resources available and profitability.

When you begin to work on your project statement, your total set of past experiences, as well as your hopes and wishes for the future, come with you. As you review the answers to the questions from chapter one, ask yourself these additional questions:

- What materials are available?

- What knowledge do I have, and what knowledge do I need?

- What resources do I have and what do I need?

- What area(s) do I want to investigate?

- What puzzle pieces before me can be turned into a project statement that fit my needs?

Once you begin to answer these questions, you must seriously think about what each part of this "project statement" means to you. This is important so when questions arise about your project statement, you have clear answers. Having clear answers helps you make better decisions because your decision will be based on whether or not the opportunity relates to your project statement, or not. This is where your project statement helps you craft your business. The statement needs to be specific enough to offer a definition of your dream, while still being open enough for your dream to evolve and for it to allow many possibilities.

For those of you who are perfectionists, understand that this is **not** a time to seek perfection. When that little voice in your head tells you that your idea is not perfect, you must discard it and believe that the time for perfection is down the road, after you get past this stage.

Daniel Pink, in his book *Drive*[1], points out that mastery is a mindset. Pink makes his point with this example: "From algebra, you might remember the concept of an asymptote. If not, maybe you will recognize it below. An asymptote (in this case, a horizontal asymptote) is a straight line that a curve approaches but never quite reaches."

---

1   *Drive: The Surprising Truth About What Motivates Us*, Daniel H. Pink, Riverhead Books, 2009

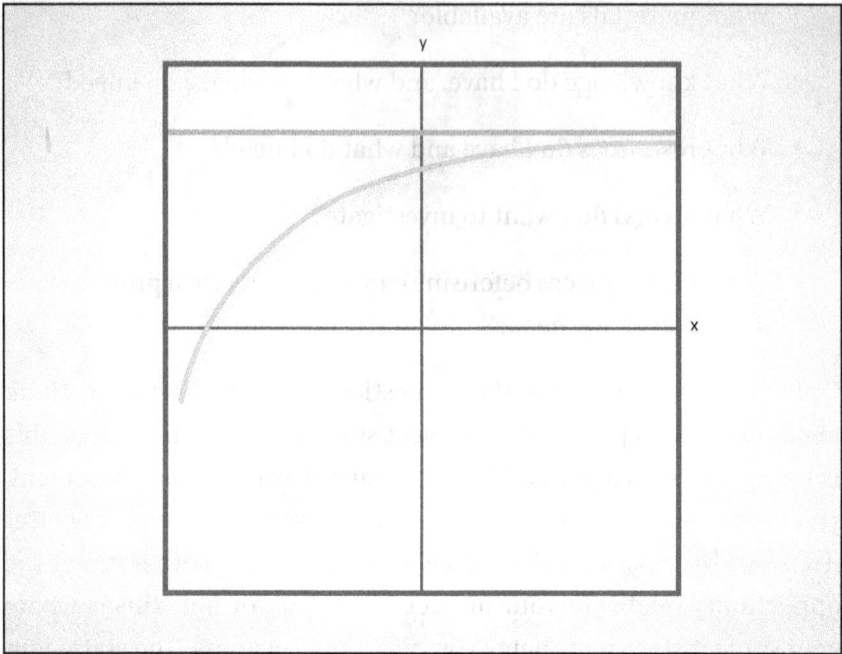

Diagram from *Drive: The Surprising Truth About What Motivates Us*
(Daniel H. Pink, Riverhead Books, 2009)

This line also summarizes the business process. Even years after your business opens, you may maintain this feeling of incompleteness as you constantly improve upon the line, but never quite hit the perfection point.

It is very important to sketch out and create different versions of your project statement before you begin to generate some initial ideas. Take your time. Don't rush the process. Write your ideas down and put them away overnight, or better yet, for at least a few days to a week. Then return to them. Reread, review and rewrite them. Let your subconscious mind work on them when you're away. Thousands of creative entrepreneurs say they get their best ideas in the shower, while playing a sport, or simply relaxing. Take time to allow ideas to "percolate" through your subconscious and up to your consciousness. Keep a tape recorder or pen and paper beside the bed in case you wake up out of a lucid dream with a great idea. Record it before falling back to sleep.

Neither great art masterpieces nor million dollar businesses happen from the first sketch. In the world of art, the great masters created sketch after sketch until their concept appeared right. Sony was not a major electronics company in the beginning. It was a small group with an idea. One of its first ideas was a rice cooker that, in the end, did not work. However, its creators did not quit. They simply drew more sketches and pursued more ideas.

Crafting happiness

As you think about developing your project statements, ask yourself, "Why I am I doing this?" What are you really looking for? Sometimes, at the core, we need to feel in control of our actions. We want to feel excitement and/or get a deep sense of satisfaction from our work.

When did you last feel satisfaction from the work you did? I would guess that last time was the last time you pushed yourself to the limit, the last time you voluntarily performed an action that resulted in accomplishing a difficult task. What you experienced was not easy, but it gave you a sense of mastery. This experience of pushing yourself to the limit and achieving success has a profound impact on your life. The resulting feeling of these experiences may well be the closest you can get to happiness. What is important to note here is that you made this happen. Oftentimes we feel less happy when the work isn't hard. Have you ever gone hiking and climbed a steep hill or trail? Did you appreciate and feel better about the exertion than hiking a flat or easy trail? We appreciate and enjoy most the things we work hard for. Look for and appreciate those challenges to your business.

What provides you with a peak experience? Think about this, as it is a very important question. As you design your business, consider what gives you the feeling of happiness, or that sparks that peak experience. Indeed, as you write the project statement, keep asking the questions: "What makes me stretch?" and "What makes this effort worthwhile?" Starting a health care business might not be enough. Maybe starting a health care business that works with terminal patients, or the homeless, or a specific population might be what you need to feel stretched and challenged.

Framing your project statement

Remember the discussion of the journey in chapter one? As you begin to write your project statement, you'll arrive at the exploration stage. You may want to review that section of chapter one about what happens during both pre-decision and exploration stages of the journey. Review your notes and your answers to the question, "What are my values?" If you plan to start something within an existing company, you need to consider the company's values, politics and culture. Do your values match theirs? Are you conflicted about their politics and culture? If your values, ethics, politics and culture don't mesh well with your existing company, consider the advantages of leaving, or explore how you can make it work in a way that doesn't compromise your own values to adhere to theirs.

Before a sketch can exist, you must have a general idea, a notion or feeling that provides you some direction. If you don't have an idea, your passion, values and interests is the area to investigate. Your project statement should capture that notion you have when you think about what you want out of life and out of a business. Again, this is why understanding yourself is critical. Your project statement is not **the** idea, but it does act as a framework for the development of your ideas. It helps give form to your sketch. The basic project statement has the following elements:

- The innovative objective to build a business, launch a product or create a new market

- State the product category: human care, snack food, employee training or others etc.

- Resources available for this project: people, time, funds, knowledge, resource, skill set

- Expected market size: Number of individuals to be served, number of corporate clients

- Time frames anticipated to allow you to accomplish these objectives:

    ° exploratory phase – three months,

    ° developmental stage – six months,

    ° implementation – two months

    ° time to profitability – two years

Here are some examples of project statements that include these additional elements:

- Develop a game for families to play. The amount of $50,000 is available to use to fund this project. Use my free time to develop. Complete this project within six months.

- Develop a service to be sold to colleges and universities to support their office of admissions services. These services will use video and journalistic practices. Use excess cash flow and equipment from existing business. The service will employ two to three people within a year and generate revenue in excess of $1 million within three years.

- Create a $50 million business within the intermodal division. Use all existing division resources but avoid creating additional capital expenditures. Complete project within twelve months and create positive cash flow within two years.

- Develop a business in "human care." Resources available include engineering, marketing and sales skills in the medical device area along with physicians who possess specialized skill sets. Limited funds are available. Time to approval and launch should be within two years.

Considerations

Before you begin to craft your project statement, there are some things to keep in mind. Consider the project statement as a framework which remains intentionally vague, as you can see in the examples above. This vagueness allows you to explore and examine the many possibilities for a business or service. At the same time it sets some boundaries on the process, such as resources and time to completion. By modifying any one of these parameters, the resulting sketch and the developing ideas can become very different indeed.

When crafting the project statement, also focus on your **ultimate** goal and include several answers about that goal. Set your answers aside for a while, and then return to them. Make any necessary modifications, and then examine them again to discover whether any should be eliminated. Consider whether any of the statements can be combined. Force yourself to whittle your ultimate goal down to one sentence, or even one word.

Creating sub-goals

After you have written a few project statements, it is time to start looking at sub-goals. These are important because they are like stepping-stones on the path toward your ultimate goal. There are literally thousands of sub-goals to choose from. Here are a few examples to prime your thinking. Be sure to read this entire section before crafting your project statement and sub-goals. Escaping the corporate grind is a typical goal, however, entrepreneurs must take care not to create their own kind of corporate grind. Make sure that what you are thinking about trying to build does not just recreate a new version of this tedium. Consider: Do your thoughts fit your values and strengths, and does your passion move you toward some kind of "in the zone experience?" Is your objective creating additional cash flow? Is your goal to develop a small business or venture that you can run on your free time, like a hobby-turned-business? Or does your objective involve maximizing your human capital in retirement by creating an income flow?

What is human capital? It is the set of capabilities an individual possesses, such as knowledge and skills, which enables that individual to perform labor that produces economic value.

Most business people today realize that human capital is extremely important. Is your objective to create a business that will act like an annuity once it is in place, helping to fund life's expenses? Do you want to give back, to fill an important need in society, like working with the underserved, or is your purpose to create a business around your passion? Write down your thoughts and list as many sub-goals as come to mind.

Create a lengthy, thorough list of sub-goals, then explore, visualize and dream. Focus on each one. Sometimes, a meandering route may be the most direct from point A to point B. What form does that ultimate goal look like today? How will it look in three years? Will it look differently in five years? What is your sense of how fulfilling these sub-goals are today? Will they feel different in three or five years? Write out as much as comes to mind.

Below is a list of questions to consider in creating sketches of your sub-goals. These questions do not require any specific answers, but merely a simple answer, such as, "a lot," or "a little."

- What would cash flow look like at start-up? At one year out? Three years out? Five years out?

- How many customers do you need at start-up? How will this differ one year out? Three years out? Five years out?

- How many sales will you need at start-up? How will this change at one year out? Three years out? Five years out?

- Keep it simple; we are just being playful here. This merely is an exercise to get a feel for the vision, drawing on many of the answers already developed.

- What product or service category fits you and your knowledge, skills, strengths and passion best?

- What resources are available for this project? Consider the list created from chapter one. Which resources fit best here? Which new ones come to mind?

- What is your time frame? Set a timeline as a guide. Most of all, keep that time frame realistic. One of my projects has a time frame of eight years, owing to legal and cultural changes, the economic situation and other unexpected events.

Finally, you are ready to begin to craft your project statement. Remember to keep it simple and consider the:

- Innovation objective

- Resources available for the project

- Time frame to accomplish the objective

Craft more than one project statement and have fun with the exercise. Do not limit yourself; stay open to the possibilities. At this point, it is about **your** intuition, feelings, desires and wishes.

Now that you have crafted a number of project statements, go back and ask the same set of questions or criteria about each statement you have crafted.

	YES	NO	MAYBE	WHY
Fits my strengths				
Stays away from my weakness				
Fits my values				
I have a passion for this area				
This area energizes me				
I can visualize myself doing this				
I will achieve peak (in the zone experience) doing this				
Gives me the opportunity to approach my ultimate goal				
Gives me the opportunity to approach my sub-goals				
Fits available resources				
Timeline is realistic				
Others goals you might want to add				

Once you have reviewed each statement, rank them. What parts of each statement do you like? Can you identify a part from each statement that can be improved?

While you ask these questions, you may find that your project statement is outside the boundaries of your criteria. Ask yourself, "How can I modify this project statement to fit those criteria?" If you modify the statement, be sure to review your criteria because, from time to time, by making one change, it will cause another part to move outside your boundaries.

Rank the statements from one to ten by the identified criteria. Review the highest-ranking project statement with someone you trust and who knows you well. Explain what you are trying to do and make sure that person understands that this exercise is very early in the process. You are not looking for specifics from the person, but are trying to set a general direction to pursue as you explore and investigate further.

Ask the person to read the project statement. Always review each set of criteria with that person and ask for an opinion about how each fits and if it sounds realistic. Listen very carefully and ask questions to clarify the answers provided. If need be, consider the feedback and make any necessary modifications. This is an iterative process; however, the effort spent here will save time in the long run.

Once you have a solid project statement and are convinced it is the best one possible, you are ready to proceed. At this time you can gather information about the potential area or areas of investigation, its customers, its environment, its offerings, etc. In general, it is best to conduct a quick overview of this area. Once you have completed this overview, it would be wise to review your project statement again and make any necessary adjustments.

Crack the left side

"It may be hard for an egg to turn into a bird, but it's harder to learn to fly while still an egg. We are all eggs at the moment. You cannot go on indefinitely being a decent, ordinary egg. We must hatch or go bad."

~ C.S. LEWIS, BRITISH SCHOLAR AND NOVELIST

Now that you have a first sketch of your project statement, it is time to determine who your customers will be. After all, without customers, you have no business. Therefore, you need to do some research to ensure that you will be able to attract customers. When you investigate the general area you have chosen, you will need to seek answers to many questions in order to guide your thinking. You may even need to modify your project statement. Most questions will revolve around customer needs, wants and demands. For the purpose of this book, below are some useful definitions for these terms.

A **customer need** is something essential to life, such as food, water, shelter, clothing, safety and esteem, to mention a few. These needs can be defined best as essential elements for human survival. If your product is a high-end sports car or a designer wardrobe, these would not be considered needs, but desires.

Innovation process flow

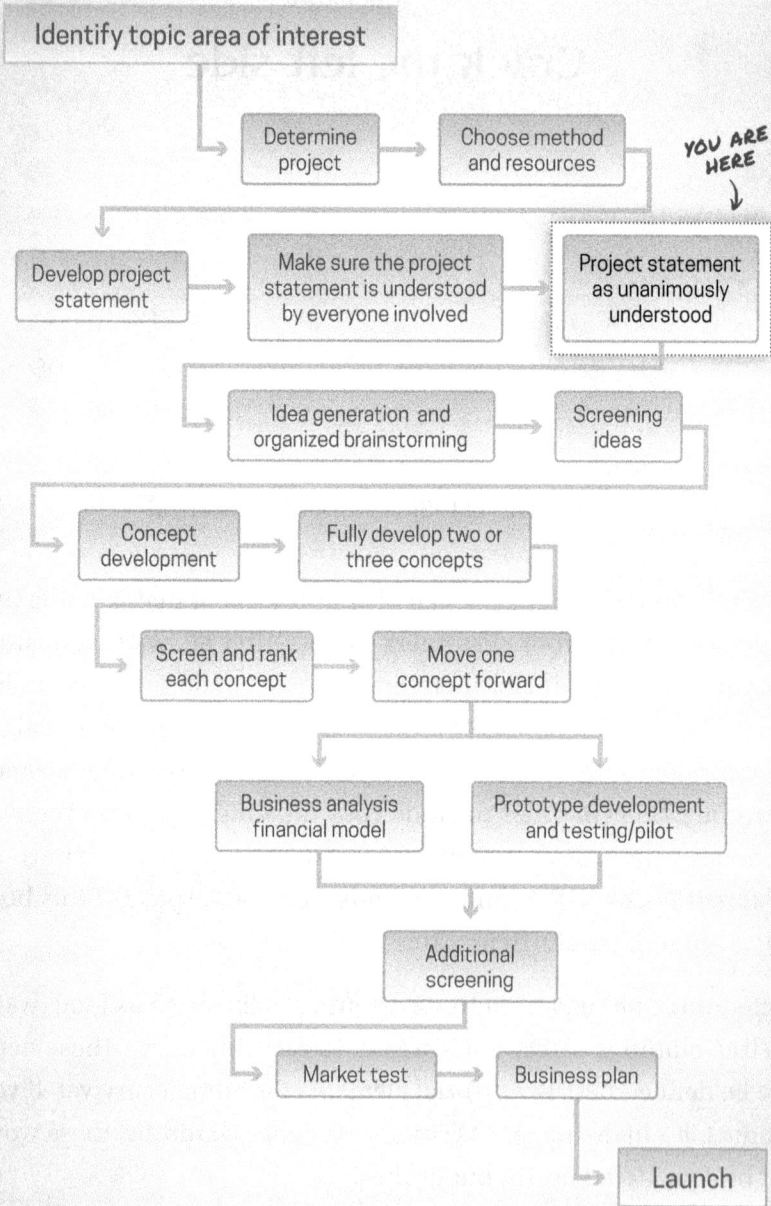

Identify topic area of interest

Determine project → Choose method and resources

YOU ARE HERE ↓

Develop project statement → Make sure the project statement is understood by everyone involved → Project statement as unanimously understood

Idea generation and organized brainstorming → Screening ideas

Concept development → Fully develop two or three concepts

Screen and rank each concept → Move one concept forward

Business analysis financial model   Prototype development and testing/pilot

Additional screening

Market test → Business plan

Launch

Consumer wants are desires for specific items that satisfy deeper needs. A want is something someone would **like** to have, even if it is not beneficial. It could even be bad to have. These may include items like a television, an iPod, a designer wardrobe or a Porsche 911.

Consumer demands are the desire for specific products accompanied by an ability and willingness to purchase them. There are many things we all want, but fewer that we demand. This is a critical differentiation point. Demand is what we need to determine during our investigation. It involves not only whether or our idea is something people want, but also how much and how often they might want it. A customer must have both the willingness and the ability to purchase your product or service on a regular basis.

Before proceeding, here are some questions to consider as you read this chapter. Just consider them as you continue to read, then go back and answer them in your notebook when you complete this chapter.

- What do you want or need to know?

- What exploratory work do you need to do?

- What trade shows do you need to attend?

- What publications do you need to investigate? What books, publications and periodicals do you need to examine?

- What additional Internet search is required?

- What trends or megatrends are evolving or becoming evident?

  ◦ Which of these trends loosely fits your project statement?

- Is there a consistent customer need?

  ◦ Have you talked to potential customers?

- What do customers want?
  - What are your customers' desires or demands?
  - How much and how often do customers buy your product or service?
- How do you use the project statement to stay grounded?
- What are the needs or demands of each market segment you investigate?
- What market segments appeal most to you?
  - Who in this segment makes purchases?
  - In which demographics are these buyers?
  - Who are your competitors in this segment? What do they offer?
  - What are substitute products exist in this segment? What do they offer?

    Note: A substitute product is a product that performs the same or similar functions as another product.
- How do you plan to contact market segment participants?
- How well do the market segments you researched fit your project statement?
- How well do the investigated segments fit your personal criteria checklist?

Discovering customer needs and wants

There are many ways to explore the needs and wants of your prospective clients. If you currently have an established business, existing customers are a great source of information. If you are an individual, you may or may not have direct access to the potential marketplace. If that is the case, at this stage, you may only want to skim the surface as you do your research. There will be plenty of opportunities in the future to investigate more deeply. The next chapter will include more extensive brainstorming. If you dig too deeply into the research and data now, you may, in effect, don mental blinders, which will have a limiting impact on the brainstorming/creative stage.

To assist you with this process, as an example, this actual project statement was given to a team that represented a small venture firm:

> **"Find a business in human care, develop a business plan, and be ready to look for financing within six months. You have $50,000 available to you for research."**

Remember, you or your firm is like this venture firm. The resources you will spend in pursuit of your million-dollar business idea will be real, whether those resources are time or money.

Start with research: The importance of trends

Whether you are an individual or you have an existing business, your first step in this investigation is to use the web to see what and if you can quickly find that might fit your project statement. Do not spend a lot of time here; just do a quick Internet search. For those of you who prefer old school methods, secure a copy of the *Yellow Pages* or consult a reference librarian to see what you can find. By doing this, you will to begin to more clearly define your search criteria.

The next step on this path is to explore the environment for long-term trends. There are many places to be found on the Web. Go to the website *Ask.com* or other such sites and pose different questions, such as trend research, megatrends, or population trends, and so on. Visit different think tanks[2] and search each site for trend research. View online book-stores, such as Amazon, and search trends and megatrends to find books on this topic, like John Naisbitt's ***Megatrends*** or Faith Popcorn's *The Dictionary of the Future: The Words, Terms and Trends That Define the Way We'll Live, Work and Talk.*

Investigate these resources to discover any trend information that may emerge from the data you uncover. You may glean insights that will impact your project statement and the directions you choose to pursue. In the human care example, the trends appear to be:

- more single heads of households

- an increase in dual-income households

- extended families not living in close geographical proximity to one another

- both men and women appear to be living longer

These trends indicate a general flattening, and possible decline, in the general population, which, potentially, may impact the direction your project may take.

---

2   Enter the phrase "trends think tank" into a search engine

As you begin your research, you will need to understand these mega-trends. These are the enormous forces in societal evolution that have a high likelihood for significantly influencing all areas of life in the next ten to fifteen years. Many individuals, companies and organizations of all types study megatrends and consider them as they develop products, services and as well as overall strategies.

The information below was presented to the group working on the human care project. You may notice that megatrends are an important part of the research this group developed. As they performed their research, they looked at a number of segments - although that number in the diagram below has been reduced from many to a few. They researched the existing megatrends, then examined trends within each of their segments.

Human Care

Older adults	Middle-aged adults	Young adults	Teenagers	Children	Infants

Birth rates, aging, globalization, technological developments, prosperity, individualization, commercialization, healthy lifestyles, care for the environment, and urbanization

Trends	Trends	Trends	Trends	Trends	Trends
• Living longer lives • More active • Rising medical costs • Working longer	• Lower incomes • Supporting children longer • Low retirement savings rate • Single heads of households	• College debt • Think community • Under-employment • Connected	• Tattoos • Piercings • Tech use • Family composition/ structure	• Family composition/ structure • Single heads of households	• Lower birth rates • Decline of traditional families

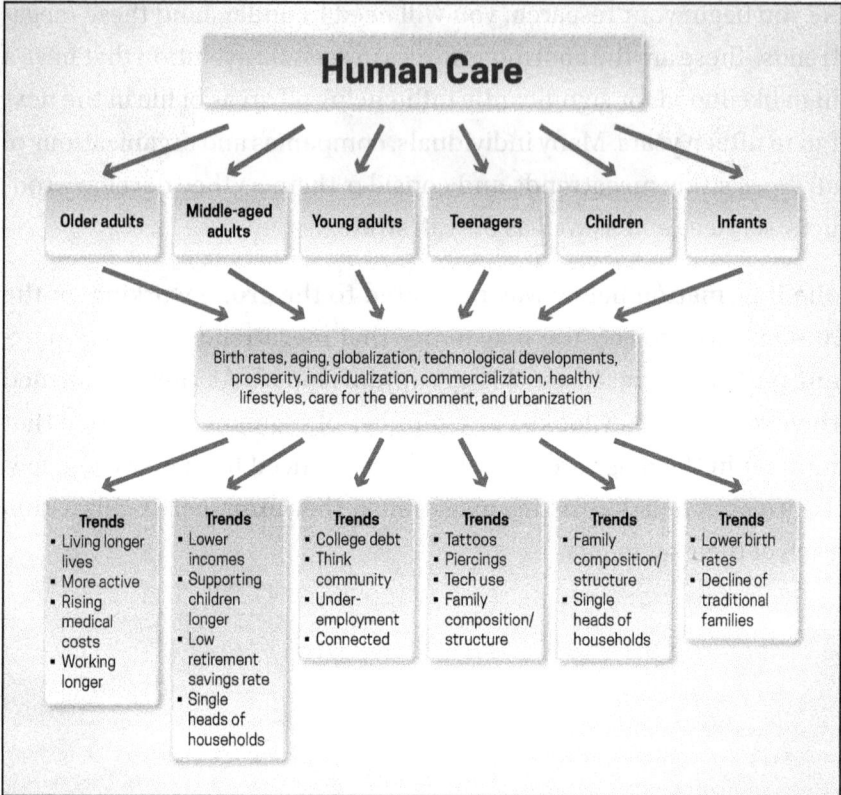

Now it is your turn. Pull out your project statement and quickly review it. What segments are now visible to you?

The goal at this point is to keep open as many potential options as you can develop. It is always easier to eliminate options when there is a greater selection. It is more difficult to discover creative alternative segments.

Next, you must do your research. Find the most current best work on megatrends. Search sites like Amazon, and use search engines for the term "megatrends," then pull together all the data. Take advantage of the resources available. Once your megatrend research is complete, take a high level look at each of your segments. Again, Web searches into each segment will yield excellent insights and information. This is the point at which you carefully inspect some of the think tanks and white papers available. Look for what is being written about any segment in which you are interested. Are there blogs, magazines, newsletters and or other materials dedicated to this segment? If so, find and read them. All new product developers share one trait: they are voracious readers, not just in their own fields, but also in fields related to what they do.

To assist you in understanding and organizing the megatrend information that could impact your business idea, a megatrend template is provided in Appendix A.

As you begin your research, notice the different phases of marketing research: exploratory, descriptive and causal. The first phases of research discussed below are the exploratory and the descriptive stages.

During the exploratory phase, the problem is unknown. For example, we know that we are looking for a business in human care. However, we have no idea what that might entail, or what segments, if any, are a fit. We seek a definition and understanding around the dimensions of our project statement. Once we have gained a better understanding, we will be able to set a more realistic course of action.

In the descriptive phase, develop a set of possible directions - such as in this human care example, which could be, "One end of a spectrum for home care that includes care for the elderly, while the other end of the spectrum would be home care for newborn babies." Once a few general directions have been chosen to explore, you may ask questions like:

- What is the market size?

- What important demographic questions need to be asked?

- Who are the buyers?

- Who are the competitors in the general space?

- Where are the holes, the areas not being serviced?

The questioning should be aimed to find out the who, what, were, when and how of the topic.

Quickly, search the Internet for whatever segment or segments you have identified. In this example, during this search, you will find a wide range of possibilities from elder care to newborn care, and from high technology companies to very low technology companies and others. Depending on your skills and knowledge, you may well find a lucrative, open space in which to create this particular business.

Identifying a promising opportunity

A "promising opportunity" is best defined as an intersection between a trend and one's ability (strengths) to deliver what a customer needs, wants and desires. As you work toward identifying an opportunity that is promising for you, here are some questions to consider:

- What trends do I notice that loosely fit my project statement?

- Who are the people who write or talk about my potential target?

- Does anyone else offer a similar product or service?

- Are there opportunities to talk to potential customers?

- What trade shows do I need to attend?

- What publications should I investigate - books, websites, bloggers, publications and/or periodicals?

- What additional Internet research should I do?

If you are already in a business within the segment you have chosen, gather information from your customers first. What are they asking for? What are they not getting from existing products and services that they'd like to receive? What does your competition offer them? If you are losing customers, ask them why they are leaving. Ask a variety of employees what **they** identify as customer needs and wants. If you have a sales force, query them. They are your best line of communication about current customers and should be able to provide a solid assessment of the existing situation.

You also may have developed channels. A marketing channel moves goods and services to customers. These channels, to name a few, include wholesalers, retailers, brokers, manufacturer's representatives, sales agents, transportation companies, independent warehouses, banks and websites.

If you are an individual, you will need to find current segment customers, marketing channel representatives, wholesalers, retailers, brokers, manufacturer's representatives, sales agents, transportation companies, independent warehouses, banks and websites (consolidators). Make sure you speak to enough people to get different points of view from at least two or three of these areas, then expand your exploration from the data you gather from these conversations.

If you consider pursuing a business segment with which you are already familiar, you already will know people involved in that segment - either directly or as suppliers or as channel partners. If you do not know people in the subsection, it is time to expand your network. Identify people who can introduce you to others in that business segment.

At this point, it is very important to keep your project statement available. You will need to present this statement to others in order to learn their general ideas. It is also a good way, when talking to your network, to help identify appropriate people with whom to have productive conversations.

Remember, you are looking for promising opportunities. You may even want to get out and question customers yourself. Deforest Jackson was, at one point, the Director of Communications for Coca-Cola USA in Atlanta. Once a month he'd put on the uniform of one of the delivery drivers and accompany him on his route, pretending to be a new hire. He got a first hand view not only of the drivers and stores, but of what customers, vendors and the process was like for everyone involved. No one saw him as "management," which gave him a chance to find out what was really needed, and just what people told him was needed. He recounts the days he spent hauling cases of sodas into stores as the best research he ever did. You can do the same – become the consumer, or customer for your product, or that of a competitor and see for yourself what the buying and/or selling process is like.

The research you undertake at this point is meant to help you gain a greater understanding of the general segment you defined in your project statement. You are not looking for "the answer." You're looking for insights, experiences, examples and data, both factual and anecdotal. This answer will be uncovered by developing the right set of questions – by gathering, analyzing and interpreting the information. You need a solid understanding of trends, market environment and problems that need solutions, as well as provide opportunities. But don't leave out the human element. All the research in the world could never have predicted the amazing success and demand for the "Pet Rock" of the 70s. The Pet Rock craze came about after creator Gary Dahl spent an evening in a bar listening to his friends complain about their pets and all the things they had to do to take care of them. He joked that a rock would make the ideal pet, that it wouldn't have to be groomed, wouldn't die, wouldn't get sick, chew up your shoes, be disobedient or need to be walked twice a day. The more he thought about it, the better the idea seemed, so he created an entire packaging and a 32-page how-to manual for caring for the rock and sold the entire package as, "A pet rock". He grossed approximately $2 million dollars during the six-month craze.

For your research to be effective, it must be timely and accurate. Old or outdated data does you little good. You are investing time and money to obtain this information, so be sure your decisions are informed, conscious and wise.

Once you complete your investigation of megatrends and segment trends, you may have a better feel for which segments you want to explore further. Take a moment and step back. Review your thinking at this point.

First, review your project statement. Does the segment fit? Does the segment feel right to you? Does the project statement itself seem right, or does it need to be altered?

Step 2: Review the work you did back in chapter two on your personal criteria. Take a look at the segment or segments that seem to draw your energy or your attention. Does your criteria checklist fit with the segment(s) you have chosen?

Personal Fit Template (Template available in Appendix B) (what are the steps to take after going through this list?)

	YES	NO	MAYBE	WHY
Fits my strengths				
Stays away from my weakness				
Fits my values				
I have a passion for this area				
This area energizes me				
I can visualize myself doing this				
I will achieve flow (optimal experience) doing this				
Gives me the opportunity to approach my ultimate goal				
Gives me the opportunity to approach my sub-goals				
Fits available resources				
Timeline is realistic				
Others you might want to add				

After creating a checklist similar to this one, the group working on the human care project chose the segment of "children" for further exploration.

To date, what have you uncovered in **your** exploration of potential opportunity areas? Which segment(s) would you choose for further exploration?

Remember in chapter one when we talked about the stages of the journey? Your journey has begun. You are now in the pre-decision stage. In fact, perhaps, you may very well be in the second stage known as exploration phase, You may feel overwhelmed by the data, the task, the competition, current obligations or/and the insecurity. You sometimes just may feel fearful.

For now, be playful and get comfortable with the process. It is important to keep moving forward.

The next chapter will illustrate how to engage in active, organized brainstorming, using your project statement as well as the information you have gathered on megatrends, trends and target segments. Before you begin the next chapter, answer these questions:

- What do I need to know?

- What exploratory work needs to be done?

    ◦ What trade shows need to be attended?

    ◦ What publications require investigation - including books, publications and periodicals?

    ◦ What additional Internet research is required?

    ◦ What trends/megatrends are visible?

    ◦ What visible trends loosely fit your project statement?

- What is a customer need for this segment?

    ◦ What potential customer feedback has been provided?

- What are customer desires and demands?

    ◦ How much how often do current customers make this kind of purchase?

- How is the project statement keeping you grounded?

- Which needs or demands within each segment need further investigation?

- What market segment(s) most appeal(s) to you?

    ◦ Who are the buyers in the segment(s)?

    ◦ What are their demographics?

- Who competes in this segment(s)? What do they offer?

- What substitute products are available in this segment? What do they offer?

- How do you plan to make contact with buyers and sellers in this market segment?

- How well do these investigated market segments fit your project statement?

- How well do these segments fit your personal criteria checklist?

Crack the right side

"Being born in a duck yard doesn't matter,
especially if you are born of a Swan's egg."
~ HANS CHRISTIAN ANDERSON, AUTHOR

Once your left-brain analysis is complete, it is time to become really creative, to take all the information collected and let your imagination run wild. In your project statement, you should have included a baseline for your creativity that incorporated any important parameters to follow. Unleash your creativity within those parameters and you will really start to focus on your million-dollar business idea.

Organized brainstorming

Here are some questions to help you shift from left- to right-brain thinking.

- Does my project statement fit my project?

- Have I identified two or three market segments to explore?

- What guidelines should I follow to successfully organize a brainstorming session?

Innovation process flow

Identify topic area of interest

Determine project → Choose method and resources

Develop project statement → Make sure the project statement is understood by everyone involved → Project statement as unanimously understood

YOU ARE HERE →

Idea generation and organized brainstorming → Screening ideas

Concept development → Fully develop two or three concepts

Screen and rank each concept → Move one concept forward

Business analysis financial model   Prototype development and testing/pilot

Additional screening

Market test → Business plan

Launch

- What is the best structure or framework to use?

- What roles must be played by those involved to ensure a successful organized brainstorming process?

- How do I avoid the normal or mundane?

- What guidelines (strategies) exist to stimulate the right side of the brain?

- How do I create fresh thinking that delves into the creative and innovative?

Organized brainstorming requires you to think differently. You must set aside all your assumptions about the world, suspend all your beliefs and set your mind free to explore. This world you are entering has no rules. There is no right, no wrong, no crazy and no sane. This is a world of imagination and vision, a world of the Mad Hatter and White Rabbit. This is the world of the subconscious. Pay attention to your intuition and to any 'hare-brained' ideas or schemes that may arise. Remember the "Pet Rock"? Listening to people's conversations and complaints is one sure way to tap into an entire universe of ideas.

Daniel Pink in his book, *A Whole New Mind-Why Right-Brainers will Rule the Future*[3], writes that our society and economy, currently built on the logical and linear foundations of the computer age, are moving into a new phase. They are being transformed into an economy and society built on the inventive and big-picture capabilities. The argument stands that these two elements always have existed and, indeed, need to coexist in order to bring products and services to market. One element may lead for a while, while the other plays a subordinate role. As with

---

3   *A Whole New Mind-Why Right-Brainers will Rule the Future*, Riverhead Books, Daniel Pink 2005

all things, the cycle changes and, with time, the roles reverse. Right-brained activity always has been the key to innovation and creation in the early stages of any product or service.

Will Gaulin, a good friend and colleague, is an expert at preparing for and facilitating organized brainstorming sessions. Each of his numerous, successful innovative projects begin with sessions lasting two-and-a-half-days.

You may wonder: exactly what is an organized brainstorming session? It is an effort to follow a free-flowing creative process in a structured manner in order to accomplish a given task.

What general guidelines apply to an effective group-organized brainstorming session?

- Create a clear project statement

- Determine a leader or project owner

- Appoint a facilitator with experience in idea generation

- Appoint someone as a recorder

- Allocate a significant amount of time

What general guidelines are necessary to create your own individual sessions? These require you to:

- Create a clear project statement

- Be able to play multiple roles-project owner, facilitator and recorder

- Use tools, such as "Mind Mapping" software, must be available for your use

- Understand how to organize the brainstorming process and how to use different thought-provoking techniques and tools

Stripping problems out of your creative process

Gaulin would direct you to check your "thinking stance." What does that mean? It means you need to consciously get into the proper frame of mind to stay focused on the project statement. It involves stripping out any problems you may face during the creative process. Head problems off before they begin.

Group facilitators always begin each session with ice breaking exercises. Why? The answer is simple. They prepare the individuals in the group to be physical, to become mentally engaged in the project, and to be psychologically connected to the other participants as well as to the facilitator. To check your thinking stance also means you need to check at the door many of your tried and true types of thinking – the safe options. An unconscious mind spends little, if any, time on that kind of thinking. Therefore, you need to file away all of your "shoulds" and "oughts" away in a mental drawer. If you do not, this thinking will severely inhibit, if not totally block, your creative, innovative, intuitive thinking.

There is one certain way to prevent you from reaching creative breakthroughs – staying on well-traveled routes or the proverbial interstate highways you know so well. These routes are wide, well marked with wide shoulders and numerous rest stops. In most cases, they are the most direct route from one location to the next and are fairly predictable, even when exogenous variables are added.

In some ways, pushing to closure can do the most damage to the creative process. For some areas and situations in life, it is important to push to closure quickly. When working on ideas that involve creation and innovation, a much better approach to the creative process is allow ideas to meander, like the bubbling brook, which gently winds through the woods. Take time to explore ideas that get your attention. See where they might lead you if you let them.

In our "hurry up and get it done" mindset, we all work within tight time constraints. Completing tasks correctly and on time in our daily lives usually proves both efficient and profitable. We always look for closure. However, to crack the right side of the brain, a push to finish quickly will offer the opposite impact. Good ideas sometimes may appear quickly, but try to avoid the pitfall of immediately accepting them entirely. Instead, continue to explore these ideas in more depth. As you drill down, additional ideas will begin to surface. Each of these will need to be explored in greater depth. Like when creating a fine wine, you cannot rush this process.

> Creativity is piercing the mundane to find the marvelous.
> ~ BILL MOYERS

The creative process should also be about striking out on your own rather than following someone else's lead. Traveling clearly marked, well-designated routes will not get you to a new place or goal but instead will take you to the same "safe" destination each time. The tried and true will never get you to the new. Therefore, get off the main road or old trail and explore your surroundings. Wander without directions or a guidebook. Seek your own way, your own path.

Seek out the surprises. Look for new, unproven changes, everything you can find, even if you think it impractical, strange, unrealistic and inefficient. Be playful, have fun, and experiment with the project, yourself, and anyone else who is on this adventure with you. Yes, this is an adventure and the more exciting and different it is at this stage, the better. If you can't get away from what you know, talk to someone who has no idea what it is you do and see what questions and insights and ideas they have. That conversation may spark something in your creative brain.

Think like a child

How, then, do you move toward a more creative and innovative "thinking stance?" You first must be creative and innovate. What does that mean? It means you must take risks. Let your mind wander and be open to all potential paths in thinking. Take the meandering route. Avoid the signs posted by others.

From my experience, people have a tendency to block any thoughts they consider risky, even when these thoughts are still inside their own heads. Stop this. Let your mind be free to wander. Allow it to travel down many paths, even those that may seem ridiculous, strange or just downright odd. Often, the best, most interesting ideas appear from those paths.

Instead, you approach cracking the right side of the brain with child-like enthusiasm. Children are naturally curious and do not adhere to limits. Everything is possible. Most importantly, everything is simple, and often very obvious. Allow yourself to become amazed and wonder out loud. Use your imagination. What do you think these children are "seeing," dreaming about, imagining? This is the kind of thinking that gets you to new places. If you can't "think like a child" then find some children who can. Ask friends, family and even a school or librarian for help. Conner Christian, age 13, got tired of having to climb in the back of his father's muddy pick-up truck bed to retrieve the tall rubber boots they wore on their farm. So he invented the "Rubber boot buddy," as a simple device to secure rubber boots to the inside wall of the truck. He went through several versions of the device before settling on an aluminum construction. His invention won first place and a hefty scholarship for Conner. His device wasn't complex and has no moving parts. Conner was simply able to see a solution where adults had not.

Be outrageous!

For other "pictures" of what it means to be outrageous, read poetry, science fiction, review works of art, try guided meditation, go on a mental adventure, and observe the world through different filters to name a few ways you can achieve this. Dig into the biographies of some of the most outrageous people out there who have succeeded when people thought they were crazy. Gary Vaynerchuk, an immigrant from the Soviet Union, and the son of a liquor storeowner, believed that the common man and woman wanted to be able to enjoy wine. But they wanted to try and enjoy wine without feeling intimidated by the traditional snobbiness and exclusivity of wine connoisseurs. So in 2006 he hosted a video podcast featuring wine reviews and advice on wine appreciation and wine related topics that were funny, realistic and appealed to the ordinary person. Instead of talking about bouquets, acidity, aftertaste and aroma, Vaynerchuk would say, "these wines tastes like wet dog hair smells," or, "Tastes like playground dirt." He was loud, funny and irreverent. Many people are intimidated by wine, and selecting the right kind of wine. Vaynerchuk made wine accessible and fun for the ordinary drinker and the new wine connoisseur. Ultimately the show was watched by more than 90,000 people and jumpstarted his business into social media.

To jumpstart your right brain's creative, innovative side, you too need to be a daredevil. That means, for a while, you must become someone who is reckless, bold, impulsive and maybe even irresponsible, to jump start the creative process. The worst you can do is fail and have to try again.

Live in the moment. Do not rush to conclusions nor force a conclusion. Used here, the definition of a moment is not merely a few seconds, but rather a significant period of time. During a recent project, the "moment" took three days but was well worth the wait. What emerged from this pause was the solution that the group had been seeking for three weeks.

Note: If you are working on the project by yourself, be aware of the potential trap many of us have. We tend to place our own meaning upon everything we see or think about. You have done this throughout your entire life, we all have. Young children have far fewer experiences with this and, therefore, have attached less positive or negative meaning to most things. To be childlike means to strip meaning and perceptions from things and create a whole new meaning/reality/illusion or perception.

Push the creative process further

Another way to really push your creative side is to ask odd questions from different points of view. For example, if you are working on a new fishing lure, one question might be, "If I was a fish, would I like that color or that shape or how the lure moves in the water?" Or, you might take an even different tact, like Mike Clark, a fireman in Alexandria, Louisiana did. For years the Crème Lure Company in Tyler, Texas had been trying to find a way to make their very popular lure, the Crème worm, float better. They'd tried everything they could do chemically, (the accepted best practice way to make things lighter in the lure industry) but the chemical process always altered the worm's color and texture. It took someone outside the company, an ordinary fisherman who didn't know that the best way was chemical, to figure it out. Mike Clarke had been trying to find a way to make the Crème worm lighter too. His solution? Simply inject pure air into liquid plastic. So he figured out a way to do just that. The Crème company looked at his process, bought the patent and now the Crème worm is more popular, lighter, and successful than ever. Sometimes it just takes an outsider who doesn't know the rules to find a solution.

How would you answer the question about making a lure better? Speculate. Identify the elements of your task and collect data from things you hear and observe, as well as from what you think and feel about these observations. Once you begin to collect your speculations, the next phase is to branch out.

I have discovered that this art of branching out is one of the most effective methods for finding, developing and recording different paths. I like to call these paths "rabbit tracks." Some of these tracks really do go somewhere while some lead to dead ends. Others loop back to the beginning. This method helps you discover the idea's many branches and leads you closer to your goal. I have found that there are a number of software programs and Apps available that are very valuable in facilitating the branching out process. Just search for brainstorming. A quick personal search quickly popped up the Apps iBrainstomer, iBlueSky. Enter the word "mindmapping®" and you will bring up the Apps iThoughtHD, SimpleMind, and MindNode among others. Any one of these Apps will assist you in your branching out efforts.

It also helps to look at some of the strategies used by innovators, such as:

- Challenging basic assumptions. For example, at one time railroads provided a great deal of long-distance passenger traffic, but today there is less railroad traffic, with the majority of that now handled by Amtrak. What if railroad companies challenged the basic assumption that they were only in the railroad business and, instead, believed they were in the people transportation business? What might happen differently? Could you find yourself on a flight aboard Santa Fe Express Airlines?

- Start from a mistake. For example, some of the most popular and well-known items in most offices and homes evolved from a series of accidental occurrences or mistakes. For instance, the 3M Post-it™ [4], The lubricant WD-40, and even White-Out for covering up typewriter and printing errors on paper were all accidents. For more information about the 3M Post-it™, visit this website.

- If you sketch these ideas, some sketches will look downright crazy. However, without them, and without trying a different approach after each mistake, the Post-it™ note would not exist. Neither would White-Out, or WD-40. In fact the name "WD-40 stands for the number of failures it took before the inventors found the right mixture for what they wanted – 40. Look for "mistakes" from which you can build and create new options. Explore the analogous. What do you find that is similar but not the same? What other businesses, products or industries are similar but not identical? Is there something that a mistake ruins that could be fixed by a new product? Think about all aspects of the product or business. In order to better use the right side of your mind, you need to consider ideas you otherwise may think of as totally irrelevant. Describe your perfect day. Delve into your mind to

---

4   http://www.vat19.com/brain-candy/accidental-inventions-post-it-notes.cfm. To read more about WD-40 visit http://wd40.com/about-us/history/. Read more about White-Out here: http://inventors.about.com/od/lstartinventions/a/liquid_paper.htm

locate your favorite vacation spot, and then place yourself in that spot, but in a different form - such as a sponge, a tree, a train, or any other object. Now, ask yourself a few questions like how do you feel? What do you see? What do you hear? Recording all the output, then review it and relate it back to your project. This should provide you with a completely different view.

- Look for what others do not see. When Bette Nesmith Graham, an artist, couldn't find work as an artist she began working as a secretary. A single woman with a child to support she took pride in her work. She wanted a better way to correct typing errors. Being an artist she realized that artists often painted over their mistakes on canvas and thought, "Why not do the same on paper?" She mixed some tempera paint with water, and began painting out her mistakes. Her boss never noticed the mistakes were painted over, but other secretaries did. They began asking her to give them some of her solution. She dubbed it "Mistake-out" and started giving it to other women in her office. Soon, the demand became a business. There are many ways of seeing by looking from different points of view: intellectual; intuitive; what is your gut telling you; convergent and divergent; and analytical and relational, to name a few. For a complete list of these parallel concepts, which can prove worthwhile to investigate and explore with your project in mind, see the next page. Play the what-if game. What if you already had a million dollars? How would you spend your time? What if you could solve a problem in a way no one else could imagine? Make unexpected connections and avoid the logical ones. Jump to conclusions, but not the obvious ones. When someone says, "salt," the natural response is pepper, however, you may respond with "unicorn" or something equally unrelated that just might seem crazy until your idea evolves and takes shape.

Work through the "rules"

Much has been written about "out-of-the-box" thinking. Chances are you developed some barriers to this type of thinking. Truly creative thinking is so far outside the box that you never realize a box even existed to begin with. Even though limits often exist to what individuals can do, those limits do not have to apply to creativity.

If you already work in an organization and are working on innovation, there are three things to consider about your organization. First, it has set of symbolic rules and procedures that must always be followed. Next, individuals exist who act as gatekeepers to ensure these rules and procedures are followed. These gatekeepers are responsible for allowing innovation to exist within the organization. When you work within their symbolic rules and procedures, and when the gatekeepers approve the idea, innovation happens.

Likewise, for the individual, the challenge is to identify the symbolic rules of the market segment. Know:

- What are the "normal" procedures?

- Who acts as gatekeeper(s)?

- What must be done to make innovation acceptable?

Below, the "box" represents the system/organization/market segment with its set of rules and procedures, as well as its various gatekeepers. New, innovative ideas will, for the most part, be outside of these rules and procedures. The innovators' challenge is to work through those rules, procedures and gatekeepers to make this innovation acceptable. The following image is complex, but illustrates what innovators must do to maintain creativity while also ensuring the idea fits back into the box from which it was taken.

The Innovator's Challenge

BACK
INTO
BOX

Out of the box   "THE BOX"   Out of the box

BACK
INTO
BOX

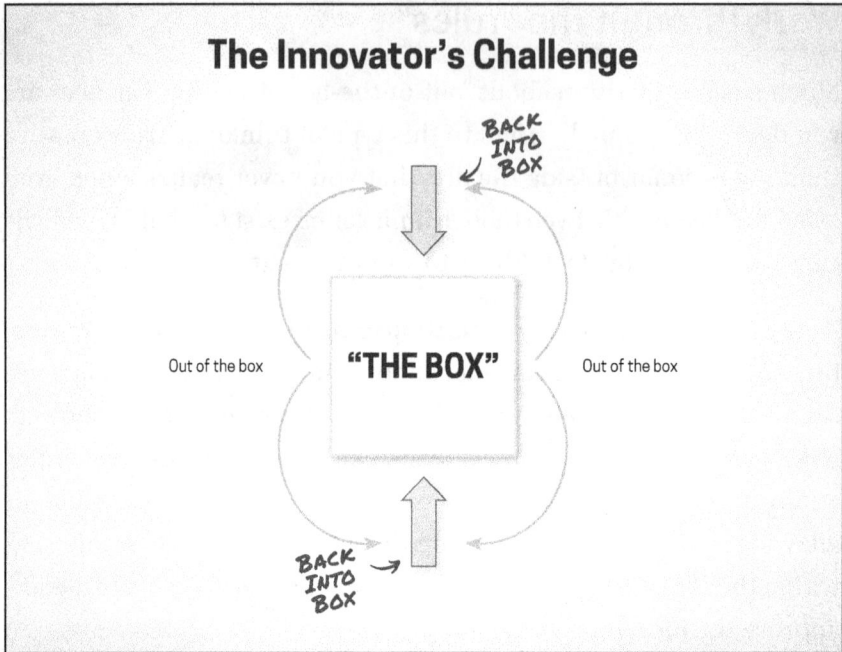

At this point, you may ask yourself if there is a system or a process to crack the right side of the brain and still ensure that whatever results is actionable. Indeed there is! Tools exist to facilitate this process as well. The rest of this book highlights some of these valuable tools and techniques.

The flowing graphic demonstrates the linear flow of the innovation process. For demonstration purposes, showing a clear, linear path helps those involved understand the process. However, be aware that, while engaged in the process, it seems anything but liner.

The Innovation Process

Time

Projected road map
Project statement
Idea exploration
Idea development
Concept statements   **Moving from
many ideas to one**
Market testing
Prototype development
Business model

Business plan development

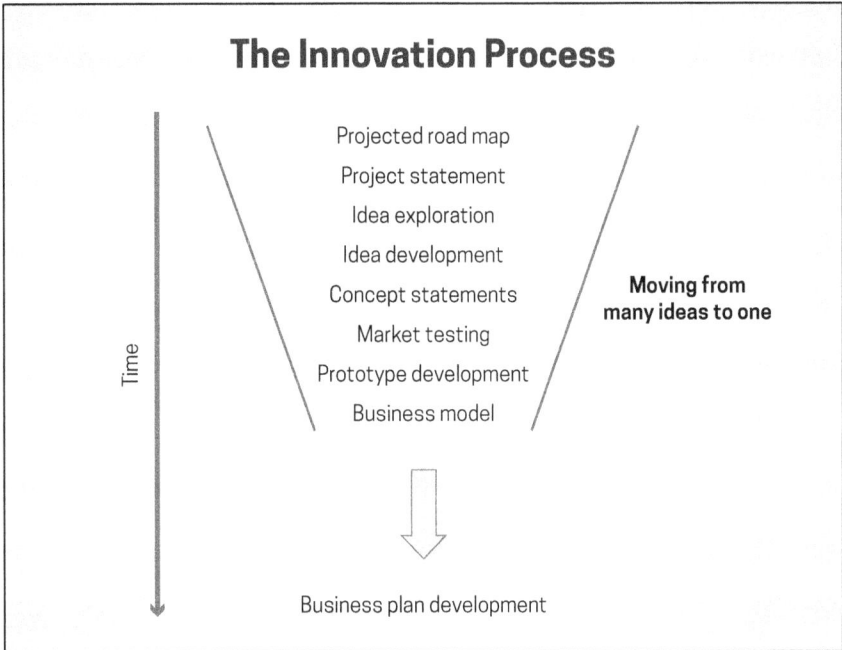

Many stops and starts are peppered with moments of going deeper; along with other moments of going back to the beginning as the process take place. This is illustrated in the chart titled "The Exploratory Stage." However, during this process, it is very important to develop idea fragments as they arise. Develop them further to produce an impact that begins with a wide-open field and narrows to an idea, which allows for development. This helps you to continually dig more deeply as you search for ideas, which, in turn, will drive you toward the creation of a concept statement.

Take a moment to review some of the important factors required to facilitate a successful right-brain cracking session.

Project statement - Remember, project statements are developed over time. A fully developed project statement should exist and be ready at this time. If you are creating this alone, you need to fully understand the statement. If, on the other hand, this is the first time a group working on this innovation sees the project statement, they need to fully understand it.

Time - As mentioned earlier, true innovation takes time, and the fastest way between two points is to meander. Take your time and delve deeply into the subject at hand.

Process - If you are cracking the right brain alone, follow this process and fulfill all of these roles on your own. If you are cracking the right brain with a group, follow these guidelines:

- Appoint a leader. This leader keeps the group focused on the project statement and redirects activities as necessary. This leader owns the project.

- Facilitate - The person who serves as facilitator keeps the ideas and conversation flowing to make sure that all ideas are considered. There are **no bad ideas** during these sessions. This facilitator also:

  - ensures that the appropriate techniques are used

  - provides stimulus at the appropriate stages

  - offers individuals assistance as they define their thinking, then draws them out as much as possible

  - sets time limits

  - works with the leader to make sure the thinking flows in a productive direction.

- Recorder - The recorder precisely captures the ideas as they are spoken and ensures the notes remain visible to the group at all times. To remain most effective, use flip charts and have plenty of wall space in order to tape comments made onto the walls.

- Introduce the project statement. As he owns the project, the leader should introduce this statement. To do this, it is best to hand it out in a written form or display it on poster board, or use an overhead visual so the entire group can view the statement. The leader will ask the group for any questions to help them understand the task at hand. Do not proceed until everyone understands this project statement. Post the project statement in a prominent place. It needs to remain visible to all throughout the right-brain cracking sessions. After this, the leader can turn the meeting over to the facilitator.

The exploratory - From brainstorming to idea generation

Of course the brainstorm exercises are merely a beginning on the road to generating ideas. Brainstorming allows for the exploration of ideas before anything concrete is settled. Ideas can begin to generate after you or the group finishes exploring. Save the ones with the most promise.

To begin this exploratory stage, use your project statement as the base for your development and set its parameters. Be sure to list the qualities of the ideal solution. As you begin your work, ask yourself or your group questions to generate proto-ideas (incomplete ideas). Use speculative and playful language. You may ask, "I wish" (I_w) and "how-to" (H_2) statements to begin. Each of these two types of statements may be incorporated into your brainstorming sessions.

"I wish" and "how-to" statements can be most effective in generating some very interesting, speculative and playful ideas. You can wish for anything. By using an "I wish" statement, you open yourself and the group to a wide range of possibilities. Some of the wildest, craziest "I wish" statements have led to the most practical concept statements. For example, while developing a new product or service for the inter-modal piggyback division of a major US railroad, one team member struck a key issue when she used the following "I wish" statement: "I wish shipping containers were like fish bowls and I could see inside."

This "I wish" statement led the team down a very different path which, eventually, developed into an innovative business concept. During this exploratory phase, the "I wish" statements can be very powerful. Here are some additional "I wish" statement examples:

Project statement: design your perfect day.

- I wish it was 72 degrees and the sky was clear all day.

- I wish I had buttermilk pancakes for breakfast.

- I wish I had a limo available to me 24/7.

The "how-to" question also brings out interesting results. While working on a product for a technology firm, I heard the following question: "How do I beam myself to multiple job and work sites simultaneously?"

This "how-to" question led the development of a highly interactive product which used radio frequency bands. "How-to" statements also have the power to generate speculative thinking and ideas. The facilitator needs to keep reinforcing the use of the speculative and playful language. Here are some additional examples of "how-to" statements:

Project statement: Design your perfect day.

- H_2 keep the buttermilk pancakes warm for an extended period.

- H_2 make daily appointments flow.

- H_2 take the edge off the day.

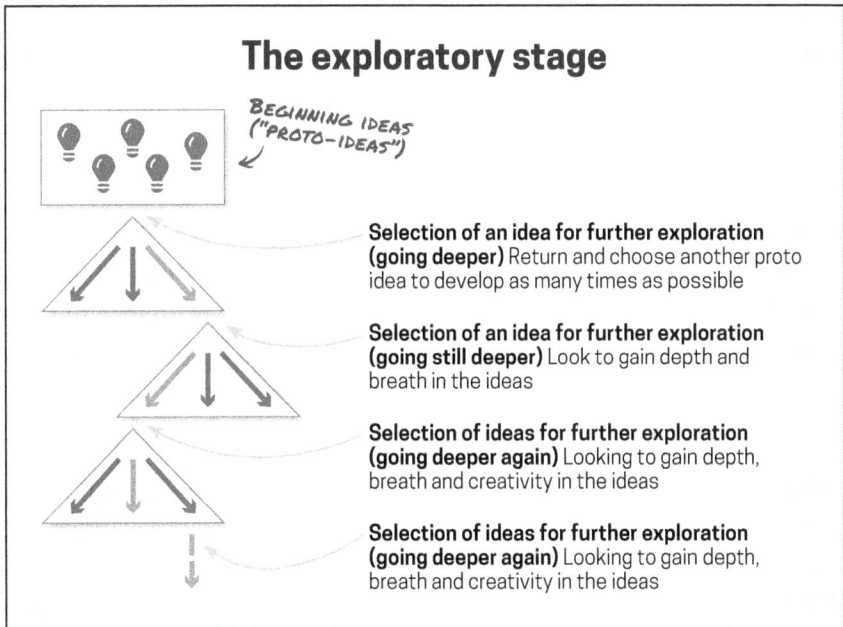

The exploratory stage

BEGINNING IDEAS ("PROTO-IDEAS")

Selection of an idea for further exploration (going deeper) Return and choose another proto idea to develop as many times as possible

Selection of an idea for further exploration (going still deeper) Look to gain depth and breath in the ideas

Selection of ideas for further exploration (going deeper again) Looking to gain depth, breath and creativity in the ideas

Selection of ideas for further exploration (going deeper again) Looking to gain depth, breath and creativity in the ideas

Collect as many ideas as possible using the two phases above. Keep those ideas visible so you can view as many as possible at the same time. Flip charts offer an advantage as they keep all the proto-ideas consistently visible. You can also use giant Post-It notes (poster size) and stick individual pages side-by-side on the wall or white board.

The time you spend on this stage is critical. Do not rush this process of generating proto-ideas. Each proto-idea is like a quick pencil sketch. It is incomplete and lacks detail. During this exploratory stage, your goal is to develop as many "I_w" and "H_2" statements as possible. These are your pencil sketches. Think about quantity, not about quality at this stage.

At the end of this exploration, the time to make choices will begin. Review at all of the proto-ideas at that time and decide which of them will be further perused.

In the case of a group brainstorming session, the facilitator consults with the leader of the project, and determines which of the proto-ideas seem to "loosely fit" the project statement. Times arise when a leader likes most of the proto-ideas or wants the group to continue on its own with little or no direction. In a case like this, the facilitator may give each member of the group five votes, allowing them to vote on their favorite ideas. No idea can get more than one vote. Once the top three to five ideas are chosen, the facilitator will go back to use the exploratory phase and further examine these three to five ideas. Once these ideas are explored and additional proto-ideas are developed, the next set of proto-ideas are selected until several possible paths have been fully explored.

The end result should be many proto-ideas. The two-and-a-half day sessions in which I participated usually led to hundreds of these "I_w" and H_2 ideas, or proto-ideas.

After this exploration is complete, it is time to expand these ideas.

The developmental stage

The ideas uncovered during the exploration state now need to be developed so they can address the project statement more fully. Several paths exist to advance to this next stage.

The path that seems to work best for me is using a technique developed during the Japanese total quality movement (TQM): the affinity diagram. This Affinity Idea Diagram[56] is a great process.

The major advantage of this diagram is its helpfulness to organize large volumes of highly participatory and incomplete ideas, or proto-ideas. It also helps to capture all the thinking so no ideas are unintentionally lost. In addition, this method allows for more thought patterns to emerge from the proto-idea data through the process of sorting and shaping.

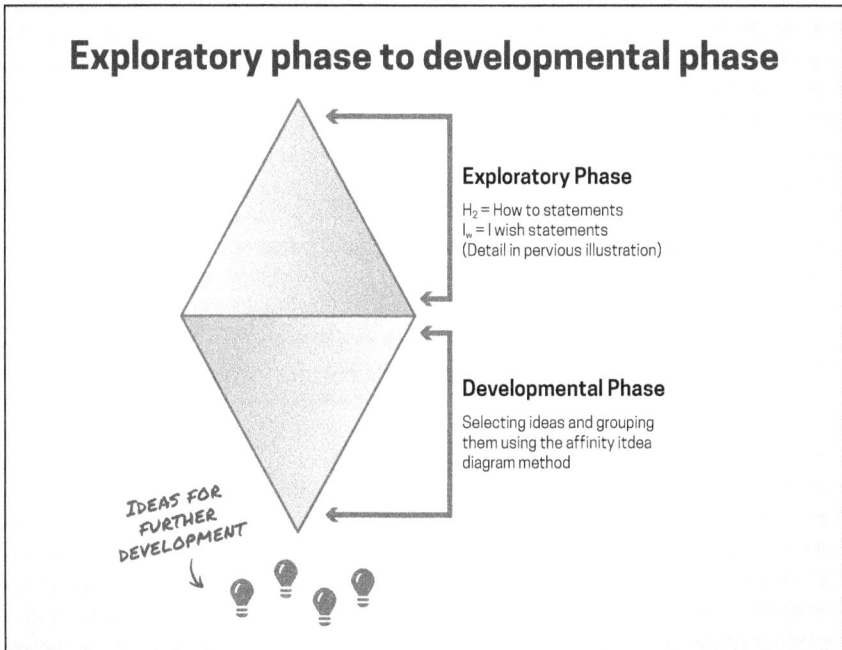

Exploratory phase to developmental phase

Exploratory Phase

H_2 = How to statements
I_w = I wish statements
(Detail in pervious illustration)

Developmental Phase

Selecting ideas and grouping
them using the affinity itdea
diagram method

IDEAS FOR
FURTHER
DEVELOPMENT

5   The diagram was created in the 1960s by Kawakita Jiro and is also known as the KJ method.
6   Improving Performance Through Statistical Thinking, Stuart J. Jamis and Jamice E. Shade, 2000 American Society of Quality Press

Here are the steps to follow when using the affinity idea diagram:

1. Review your project statement.

2. Gather the team, and supply each team member with a sticky note pad and pencil.

3. A large, flat service table is required. Remove any chairs so people can easily move around the table.

4. Inform the team that no talking is allowed during this exercise.

5. Make sure that all the proto-ideas are visible to all team members. Each person jots onto sticky notes the proto-idea(s) they like best, along with any new ideas that come to mind, randomly placing these ideas on the table.

6. After a great number of notes are posted on the table, the facilitator will ask the team members to group the notes into categories and assign a headline card to the top of each grouping. All this is done without discussion. Duplicate cards may be created for different headings. Heading cards can be changed and moved.

7. The facilitator must allow time for groupings to appear.

Here is what the process looks like:

Proto - Ideas

Project statement

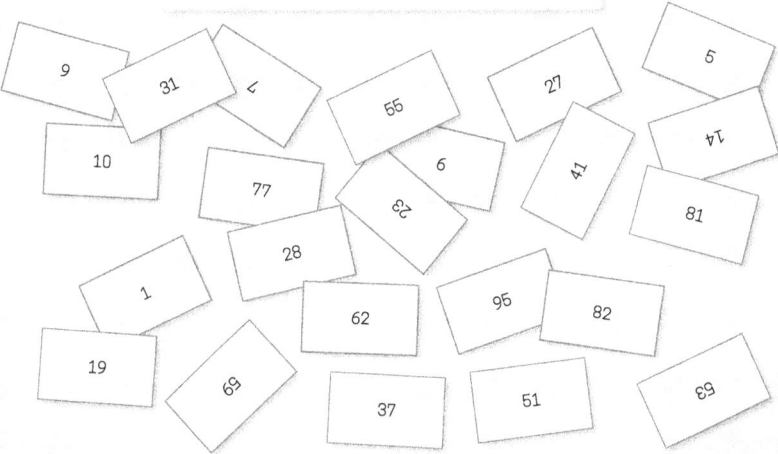

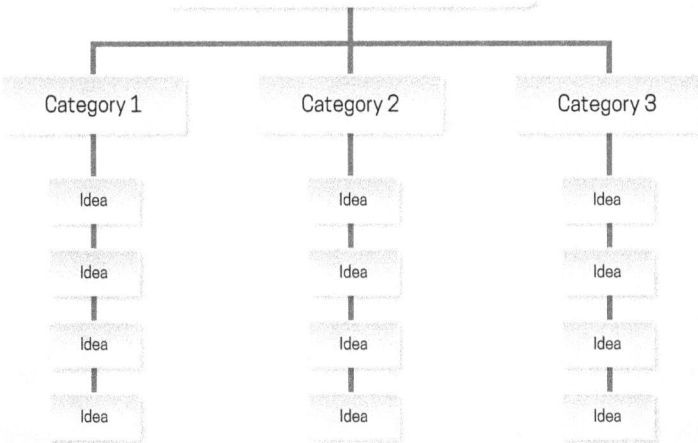

9
31
7
10
55
27
5
14
77
6
41
23
81
28
1
62
95
82
19
69
37
51
63

Affinity Idea Diagram

Project Statement

Category 1	Category 2	Category 3
Idea	Idea	Idea
Idea	Idea	Idea
Idea	Idea	Idea
Idea	Idea	Idea

Keep in mind the following process points, as you move through this developmental stage:

- Avoid easy, logical, predictable categories

- Guide your team's thinking by intrigue and intuition

  Note: One of the important actions the facilitator or group leader is asking questions and getting clarifications about thinking. The facilitator's objective is to always get the individual or group to gain more depth in their thinking. The facilitator does this by listening very closely and using questions that arouse curiosity (intrigue). Also the facilitator should use his or her own as intuition well as that of the individuals participating. Intuition here refers to keen and quick insights.

- Place the ideas into categories

- Give each category a title

Now is the time to move from a rough sketch to a clay mode phase. To make this move, evaluate each proto-idea under each category in your affinity idea diagram. This is the evaluation process:

1. Work on each proto-idea, taking one at a time.

2. List the all the possible benefits of each idea first. However, if you review the negative side first, it may prove almost impossible to return to a positive outlook.

3. Identify any obstacles that may impede implementation.

4. Work from the largest obstacles to the smallest. Develop ideas that get around or eliminate these obstacles.

5. Modify each emerging concept; use a clay model as your process moves along.

6. Outline the next steps to move the concepts forward.

At this time, you may want to review the story of the journey found in chapter one. Determine what stage of this journey you are at as you run through this process. Typically, the commitment to move ahead to create the idea your business develops during the organized brainstorming. Magical things begin to happen when you remain open. Help just seems to appear. For example, something you read or heard may or may lead to a pathway to an unanticipated opportunity or open door. Remember Gary Dahl and his pet rock? His multi-million dollar idea grew out of a casual conversation in a bar with friends about their pets. He didn't just let it go, thinking it was silly. He dug in and pursued it, as crazy as it seemed at the time. Like all creative endeavors, this part of the journey is very energizing, so enjoy it while it lasts.

Again, review the following questions:

- Can I identify two or three market segments to explore?

- What guidelines do I need to follow for a successful organized brainstorming session?

- Which structure or framework will work best?

- What roles need to be played in the organized brain storming process?

- How do I avoid the normal, mundane?

- How do I stimulate the right side of the brain?

- What guidelines or strategies stimulate the right side of the brain?

- How do I obtain fresh thinking? How so I plunge into the creative and innovative?

Below is an exercise to practice while going through this process:

Here is a project statement: Design the perfect vacation. The vacation can last between five and seven days. You should allow for a total of two travel days. At least one element should be a totally new experience for the participants. There is no budget limitation unless you decide to create one.

Take this exercise through the exploratory, developmental and affinity idea diagram stages. At the end of the process, ask yourself the following questions:

- What went well?

- What was easy?

- What was difficult?

- What else did I need to know?

- What do I need to do to gain more from this process?

Enjoy the adventure!

The next chapter deals directly with how to screen and modify ideas. Complete the exercise, "design the perfect vacation," to gain the greatest benefit from this chapter. The output from this exercise will help develop the screening models that follow.

CHAPTER 5

Develop and screen ideas

"Don't count your chickens before they hatch."
~ AESOP

In this chapter, we dive into the processes and techniques to develop as many proto-ideas as possible, and provide topic details.

By now, your ideas are probably exploding. However, if not, the exercises in this chapter will help you expand on the ideas you have. After all, you cannot effectively screen ideas if you only have a few to review.

Which screening devices are available? What can you now do with these ideas? Here is an actual example to illustrate how the idea screening process works.

At the end of the last chapter, you worked on an exercise using the project statement, "design the perfect vacation." Parameters were supplied.

Slightly modify that project statement and change the situation. After that, we will take this project statement through the exploratory process so you can follow exactly how it works. Included are a number of exercises to help you quickly expand the number of ideas you have to work with for this specific project statement.

Innovation process flow

Identify topic area of interest

Determine project → Choose method and resources

Develop project statement → Make sure the project statement is understood by everyone involved → Project statement as unanimously understood

YOU ARE HERE →

Idea generation and organized brainstorming → Screening ideas

Concept development → Fully develop two or three concepts

Screen and rank each concept → Move one concept forward

Business analysis financial model   Prototype development and testing/pilot

Additional screening

Market test → Business plan

Launch

This is your project. You, along with some of your friends, all located in a major urban area, are interested in starting a travel business. Each of you have experience in developing vacation and business travel plans, as well as the ability to find affordable ways to make a variety of vacation plans materialize. Your group is well traveled and has seen most of the world. Both you and your team feel strongly that this is the time to begin your business. You all have considered this for some time and know that a standard travel business is no longer a viable option. A mutual friend is an experienced professional facilitator. In conjunction with this facilitator, you and your group created following project statement:

Design distinct sets of vacation and travel experiences for groups. The length of each vacation experience should be between five and twenty days and its activity can range from extremely active to passive. The target age range begins at seventeen and includes anyone older. Each of these experiences should cost between $1,500 and $25,000 per individual, with everything included. The group size should range between twelve and twenty individuals. The development budget is $500,000.

With your team, use your project statement and proceed through the innovation process outlined in chapter four. Work your way through the exploratory, developmental and affinity idea diagram stages with the proto-ideas. For practice, you may want to gather some friends and hold a mini-brainstorming session to become comfortable with the process. Some process output is provided as examples. This output will become data for the screening process.

In response to requests for additional examples, here is a visual representation of the screening process.

The Exploratory Phase

Based on output from the exploratory stage session, if use the results of the I_w and H_2 statements (or the proto-ideas), they might look like the following. This, however, only represents a small segment of the proto-ideas. If you work at it, you easily can come up with more than 300 proto-ideas. Remember, proto-ideas are not fully developed statements or ideas. They are merely sketches.

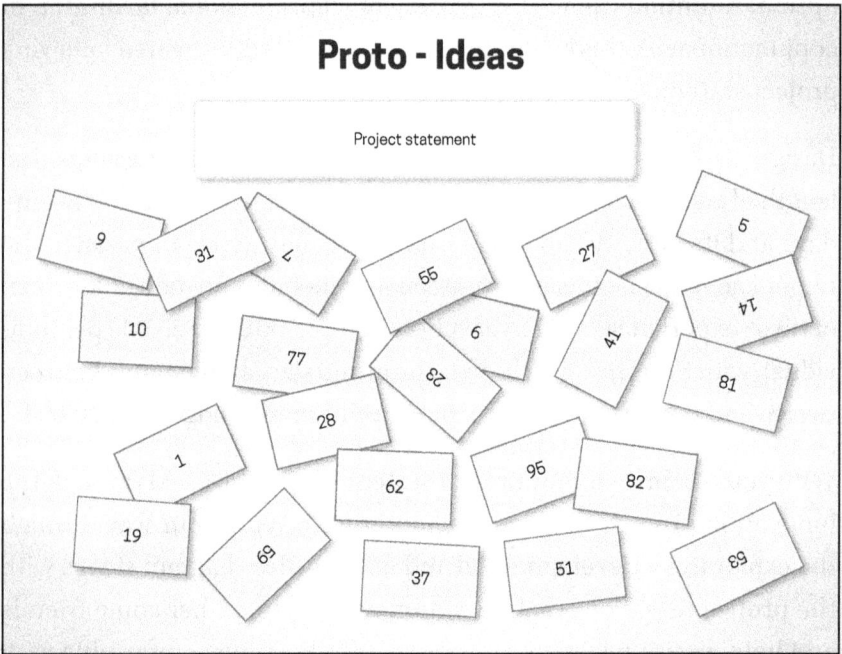

Affinity Idea Diagram

Project Statement

Category 1   Category 2   Category 3

Idea	Idea	Idea
Idea	Idea	Idea
Idea	Idea	Idea
Idea	Idea	Idea

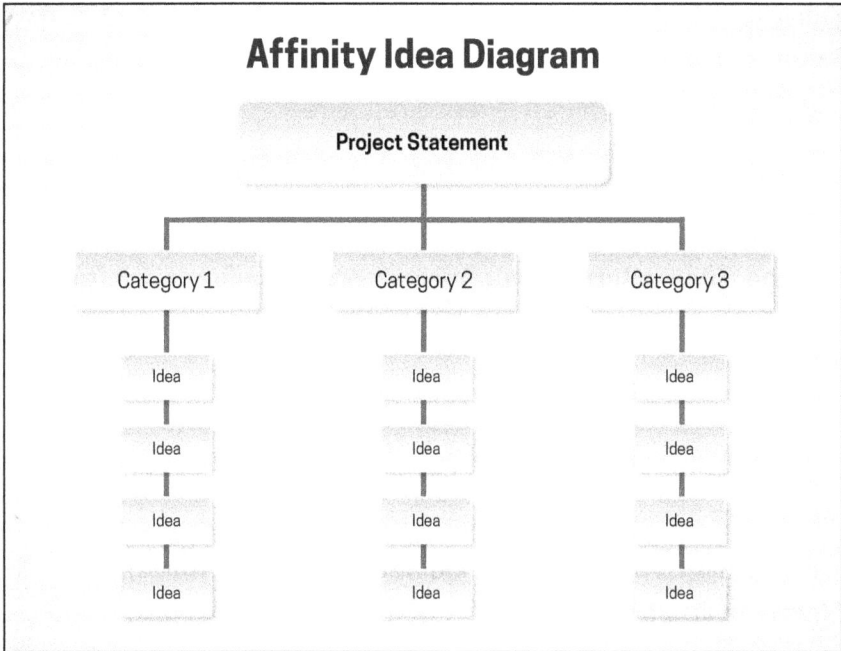

The walls, table, the sketch pad - in the case of an individual – or the computer screen, should be filled with these randomly produced proto-ideas.

At times during the exploratory phase, ideas may seem difficult to come by to may appear to dry up. If that happens with this exercise, and you find yourself without many proto-ideas to post on the wall, computer screen, or wherever you using to display them, here are some techniques you may find helpful in generating additional ideas.

Visualization

Directions:

Close your eyes and relax. Take a deep breath. You travel to a vacation spot that most relaxes you. You will spend significant time at this vacation location, so get comfortable when you arrive. What do you smell, feel, see and taste upon arrival? How do you feel after two days in this relaxing place? How do you feel when you leave this place to return home?

Write the answers to these questions in your notes.

Once again do not edit your thinking. Write down whatever comes to mind. Then, return to your session using the information from the visualization exercise to develop additional "I wish" and "how to" proto-ideas.

Metaphor

Exercise:

Develop a metaphor for life (food, vacation, relationships). Example: "Life is an artichoke."

Describe one metaphor in terms of a second metaphor, from that is born a third metaphor. Most of the time, a metaphor captures a psychological state that can only be approximated.

Try it from the other side. "Life (food, vacation, relationships) is <u>not</u> like artichoke."

Again, do not edit your thinking, but go back to develop additional "I wish" and "how to" proto-ideas using the information from the visualization exercise.

Free Association

Directions

Place a word in the middle of the circle. For example, we will use the word "money." Focus on this word for a few seconds. Insert the first word that pops into your mind and place it at the end of one of the rays – for example, the word "vacation." Go back and focus on the word money. What is the next word that pops into your mind? For this example, we will use "tuition." Place the word tuition at the end of another one of the rays. Continue this process until no additional words directly associated with money come to mind.

Then, choose one of the words at the end of these rays that grabs your attention. Repeat this exercise, replacing the word you have chosen at the middle. Repeat this exercise until you have addressed each of the words.

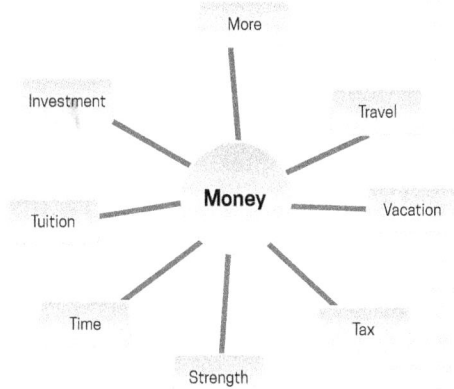

More

Investment

Travel

Money

Vacation

Tuition

Time

Tax

Strength

Write down your answers. Focus on the associations to begin to develop additional I_w and H_2 statements.

Linked Association

Money

Food

Investment

More

Travel

Directions

Using the same procedure as the prior free association exercise, place a circle in the middle of a page. Focus on the word "money" for a few seconds. Place the first word that pops into your mind at a ray. In this case, use the word "food." Now, focus on the word food you just placed at the end of the ray. Draw a line out from the word food. At the end of that line place the next word that comes to mind, for example "spaghetti." Continue this process using different words until you seem to run out of ideas. Then place a different word in the circle and create another string.

Remember, always record your thinking and review what you have written during this linked association exercise. Now, go back to the process of developing the proto-ideas using the I_w and H_2 process.

Expedition

The expedition may be an artificial or real adventure. It begins with the facilitator asking questions that require an analogical or metaphorical response. For example, you send yourself or the team to a new environment for a little adventure. The adventure could be as simple as a walk, where you each write down what attracts your attention. It may be as complicated as recording dreams, then relating them to the task at hand.

The purpose of this exercise is to focus attention away from the goal or problem. By doing this, you increase the probability of viewing a task in an uncommon or different way.

Again, do not edit your thinking, but go back to develop additional "I wish" and "how to" proto-ideas using the information from the visualization exercise.

Once again, write down your observations and focus on those associations before you return to develop additional I_w and H_2 statements.

These techniques will help to keep this exploring phase exciting, energized and productive.

The Developmental Phase

Use this specific example and proceed to the next phase - the developmental phase, which uses the affinity idea diagram. This begins with the initial organization of the large volumes of highly participatory and incomplete ideas. This method also helps to capture all the thinking revealed so far, so no ideas are unintentionally lost. In addition, this method allows for more thought patterns to emerge from the proto-idea data through the process of sorting and shaping. Remember, new ideas can be added at any time. It is also fine to combine ideas to create a new proto-idea. The following is the affinity idea diagram using the proto-ideas developed in the exploratory phase:

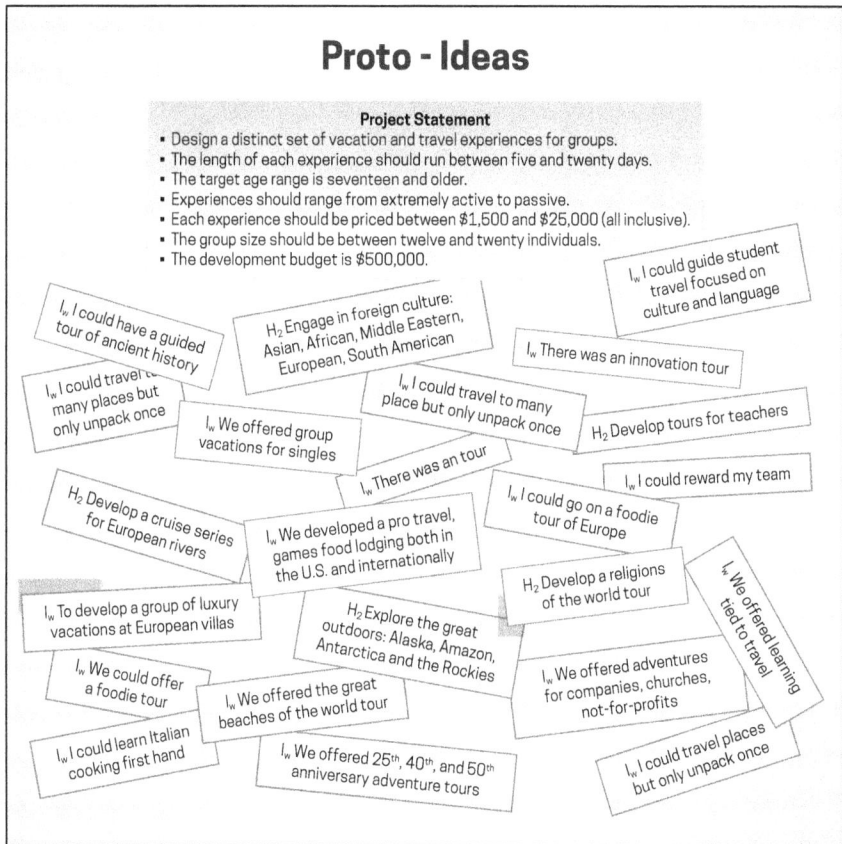

Proto - Ideas

Project Statement
- Design a distinct set of vacation and travel experiences for groups.
- The length of each experience should run between five and twenty days.
- The target age range is seventeen and older.
- Experiences should range from extremely active to passive.
- Each experience should be priced between $1,500 and $25,000 (all inclusive).
- The group size should be between twelve and twenty individuals.
- The development budget is $500,000.

I_w I could have a guided tour of ancient history

H_2 Engage in foreign culture: Asian, African, Middle Eastern, European, South American

I_w I could guide student travel focused on culture and language

I_w There was an innovation tour

I_w I could travel t... many places but only unpack once

I_w I could travel to many place but only unpack once

I_w We offered group vacations for singles

H_2 Develop tours for teachers

I_w There was an tour

H_2 Develop a cruise series for European rivers

I_w We developed a pro travel, games food lodging both in the U.S. and internationally

I_w I could go on a foodie tour of Europe

I_w I could reward my team

H_2 Develop a religions of the world tour

I_w We offered learning tied to travel

I_w To develop a group of luxury vacations at European villas

H_2 Explore the great outdoors: Alaska, Amazon, Antarctica and the Rockies

I_w We offered adventures for companies, churches, not-for-profits

I_w We could offer a foodie tour

I_w We offered the great beaches of the world tour

I_w I could learn Italian cooking first hand

I_w We offered 25th, 40th, and 50th anniversary adventure tours

I_w I could travel places but only unpack once

Affinity Diagram Example

Project Statement
- Design a distinct set of vacation and travel experiences for groups.
- The experience should last between five and twenty days.
- The target age range is seventeen and older.
- Experiences should range from extremely active to passive.
- Experiences should be priced between $1,500 and $25,000 (all inclusive).
- The group size should be between twelve and twenty individuals.
- The development budget is $500,000.

Culture/History/Education	Relationships	Fun and adventure
I w I could have a guided tour of ancient history	I_w We offered group vacations for singles	H_2 Engage in foreign culture: Asian, African, Middle Eastern, European, South American
I w I could travel to many places but only unpack once	I_w I could travel to many places but unpack only once	I_w I could travel places and only unpack once
I_w I could guide student travel that focuses on culture and language	I_w We could offer a foodie tour	H_2 Develop a cruise series for European rivers
H_2 Develop tours for teachers	I_w I could go on a foodie tour of Europe	I_w To develop a group of luxury vacation stays at European villas
I_w There was an innovation tour	I_w I could reward my team	
H_2 Develop a 'religions of the world' tour	I_w We offered adventures for companies, churches, not-for-profits	I_w We offered the great beaches of the world tour
I_w We offered learning tied to travel	I_w We offered 25th, 40th, and 50th anniversary adventure tours	I_w We developed a pro travel, games food lodging both in the U.S. and internationally
I_w I could learn Italian cooking first-hand		H_2 Explore the great outdoors: Alaska, Amazon, Antarctica and the Rockies

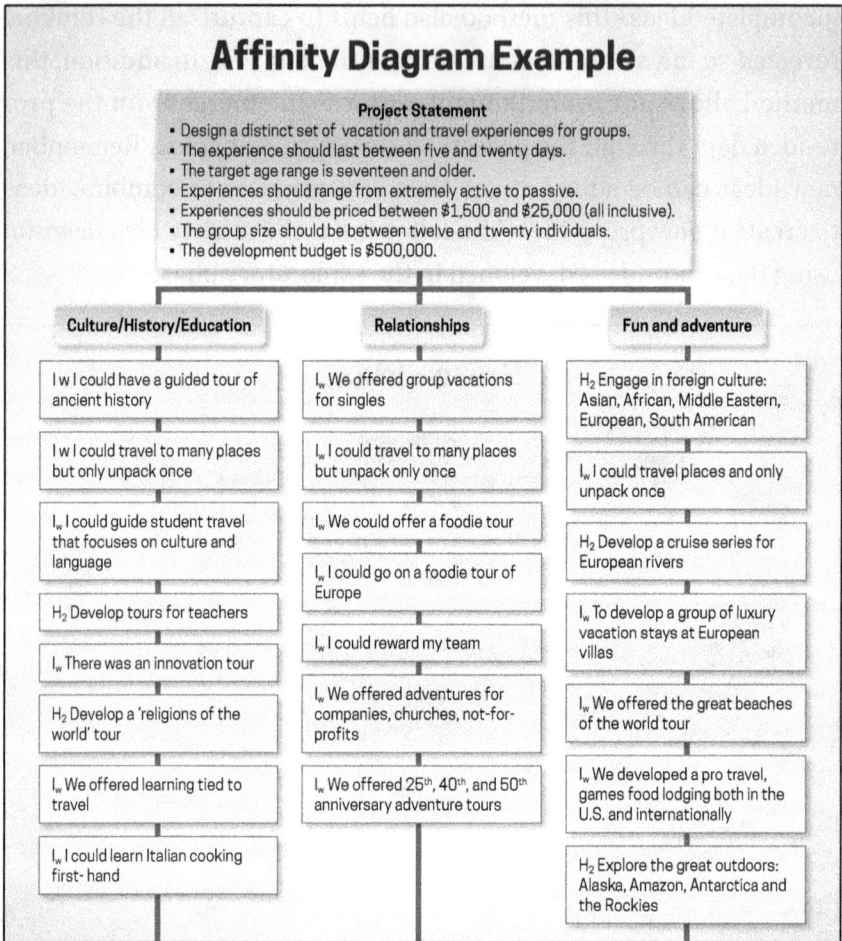

After this process, there is more work to be done, which is detailed further in this chapter (sorting, adding, grouping your Proto-Ideas and adding a headline or title card to each grouping of proto-ideas). The results in these examples are organized under an appropriate column of three headers:

1. Cultural, history and education,

2. Relationships, and

3. Fun and adventure.

If you are working independently on your own project, your groupings should be in place. You may have between two and fifteen groupings or more. This reduces the screening process to a more manageable size.

As you begin to screen each of those ideas, ask yourself:

- Does your group's or team's energy or your own, seem drawn to certain ideas more than to others?

- Can you and your team become passionate about one or more of these ideas?

- How close is the rough proto-idea to your project statement?

- How would you prioritize the opportunities?

- What are the product or service risks overall?

- Would this choice be the best allocation for scarce resources?

Focusing on one question at a time, examine each of the proto-ideas. First, go through each of the proto-ideas to determine which draws your energy and interest. Why does it draw our energy? Talk about each idea from the point of view of why it attracts you. Sometimes, to assess which of the ideas most draws your interest, you may need to allow each team member five votes. They can use their votes any way they want, and can either to use all five votes for one idea or they can spread the five votes out among five different ideas. The ideas with the most votes should be the ones discussed.

Repeat this process for each idea about which you or your team shows the most passion. Are these the same as the ideas that draw your energy/interest, or are they different ones? If these ideas are different, why are they different?

In some cases, an idea will generate both passion and energy from the group. However, once the team has chosen both the proto-ideas that most draw their energy and the ones for which they have the most passion, place them onto a table so you can visualize which ones best fit the project statement.

How closely do the rough proto-ideas match your project statement? This uses intuition. No real research or investigation took place yet. At this early stage, it is counterproductive to go further. Why? Simply stated, once you start to research, you tend to don blinders and become somewhat myopic. At this phase, the objective is to keep one's mind open to all possibilities. A lot of time remains to "get real." What is helpful, though, is to review the project statement being developed:

Design distinct sets of vacation or travel experiences for groups. The range of experiences may range from extremely active to passive. The length of each vacation experience should range between five and twenty days. The group should be limited to between twelve and twenty individuals. Pricing for the experiences should range between $1,500 and $25,000 per individual, with everything included. The target age range is seventeen and older. The development budget is $500,000.

Now break down the project statement into sections in order to view each proto-idea. Make sure it matches all the segments of the project statement or determine if it just matches some of them. Most ideas will have some matches at this stage, although some will be off base. For those that are off base, ask the question: "How can this idea be modified to fit the project statement?". This is a question will recur at each phase of the screening process. Below is a small sample screen to assist you as run through each proto-idea to determine if the ideas match the project statement.

PROTO-IDEA	VACATION	GROUP TRAVEL	5- 20 LENGTH	AGE RANGE 17 AND UP	ACTIVE ACTIVITY	PASSIVE ACTIVITY	PRICE RANGE 1K-25K	GROUP SIZE 12-20
I wish I could view ancient history	yes	yes	yes	yes	no	yes	maybe	yes
I wish my room came with me	no	no	no	no	no	no	no	no
Group vacations for singles	yes	yes	yes	yes	maybe	maybe	yes	yes
How do I take my team on an innovative tour?	no	yes	yes	yes	maybe	maybe	yes	yes
How do I develop religious travel?	yes	yes	yes	yes	maybe	yes	yes	yes
I wish I could reward my team	yes	yes	yes	yes	maybe	maybe	yes	yes
Develop a tour for specialized school groups, e.g. teams band	no	yes	yes	yes	yes	yes	yes	maybe
Develop tours for teachers	yes	yes	yes	yes	maybe	maybe	yes	yes
Rent a villa for a large group vacation	yes	yes	yes	yes	maybe	maybe	maybe	maybe
I wish I received college credit for travel	No	No	no	yes	maybe	maybe	maybe	yes
I wish I could go on a foodie tour	yes	yes	yes	yes	maybe	maybe	yes	yes
I wish ocean cruises existed for business	yes	yes	yes	yes	maybe	maybe	yes	yes

You may want to drop ideas or add different ideas to this table. For example, let your current knowledge and intuition guide you as to which ideas can be developed within the parameters of your project statement. You may want to add another section for comments and notes, as these are very important at every stage. If you add these, make sure no suggested thinking is lost which may prove helpful later in the process.

At this point, it may be best to take two or three of the proto-ideas the team has chosen and put each of those ideas individually through the exploratory and the developmental stages. This will provide a greater depth of ideas in the areas to which you and your team seem most attracted. This process can and should be repeated several times to gain the best results.

Developing screens to manage your ideas

As you continue to build the number of proto-ideas, it is important to create a system to manage these ideas. Since it is not possible or practical to advance every idea generated for further investigation, you must create a way to identify those ideas with the greatest potential. Screens need to be developed. Screen development is the process of identifying the requirements, such as regulations and success factors necessary to successfully market your product to your target audience.

The first screen chooses the idea that draws the most energy, and the second is the one for which you show the most passion. However, these two screens are insufficient by themselves as many proto-ideas probably remain.

Each subsequent screen creates a tighter and firmer mesh. Keep in mind that this new product or service development process allows for iteration. Also remember that, until this time, you have done very little research and investigation. In order to do the necessary research, investigation, concept development and testing, you need to select and examine only a few ideas at a time. If, during this process, the first set of ideas does not work out, then return to the ideas generation stage, and repeat the process using some of the other ideas conjured.

Also, it important to note that ideas that do not go make it through these screens can be modified and rescreened. Should you rescreen the modified idea, make sure to take that new idea back through all the screens. From time to time, the modification of an idea will cause the idea not to pass through one of the previous screens. If for some reason you decide not to repeat the entire process, make sure that you note why you did not repeat the process. Based on years of experience, I always recommend that all steps be repeated. Below is a diagram of how this continuous screening process looks on paper.

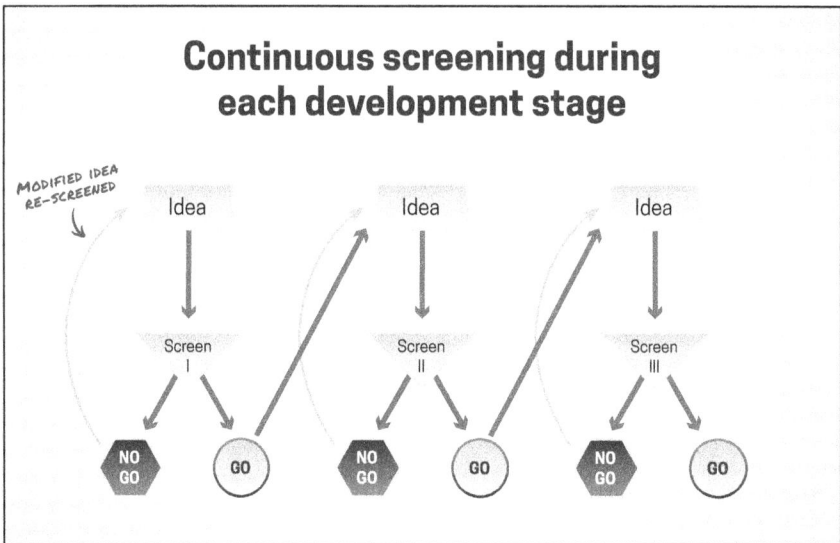

Continuous screening during each development stage

As a general guideline, once the various screens are developed, they must be applied to each idea in an identical manner.

The following flow chart shows the continuous screening process throughout the entire development cycle.

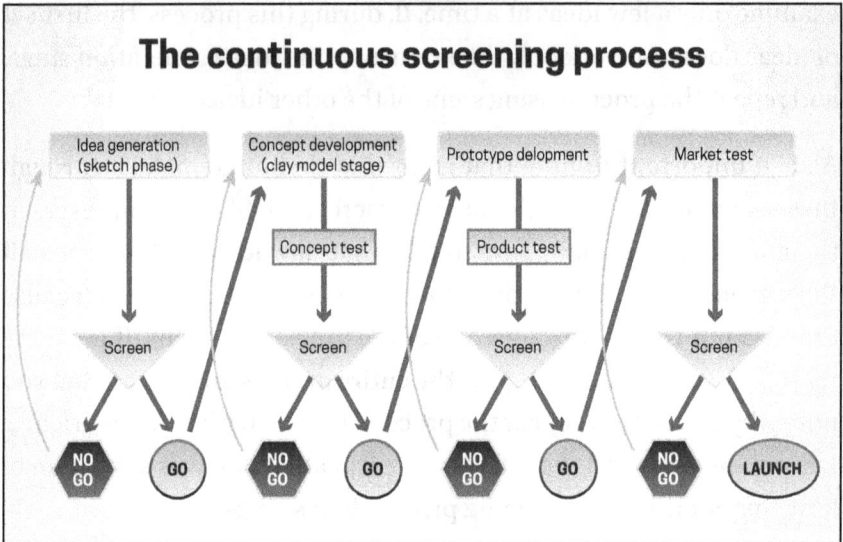

The continuous screening process

Idea generation (sketch phase)	Concept development (clay model stage)	Prototype delopment	Market test
	Concept test	Product test	
Screen	Screen	Screen	Screen
NO GO GO	NO GO GO	NO GO GO	NO GO LAUNCH

Since the first two types of screens already have been discussed, this diagram explains some of the additional screens through which you may want to run your ideas.

Typical Screening Factors

Tactical ⇨	Strategic ⇨	Business ⇨	Financial ⇨	Filter
• Degree of competition • Ability to develop product or service • Ability to support product or service • Availability of vendor/supplier options • Ability to distribute product or service • Ability to provide R&D	• Build on core competencies • Long-term growth potential • Fit with current customer base if you have one • Compatible with current sales force • Improvement in quality • Fit with current product line • Ability to develop a leadership position • Regulatory environment • Time needed for development vs. window of opportunity	• Target Market • Market Size • Market Potential • Benefits product or service offers vs. competition • Enables the customer to get the job done • Market growth potential • Product or service helps meet previously unmet needs	• Initial capital outlay • Long-term lifecycle costs • Sales dollar volume by year • Risk • Cash burn rate • Time to break-even	⇩

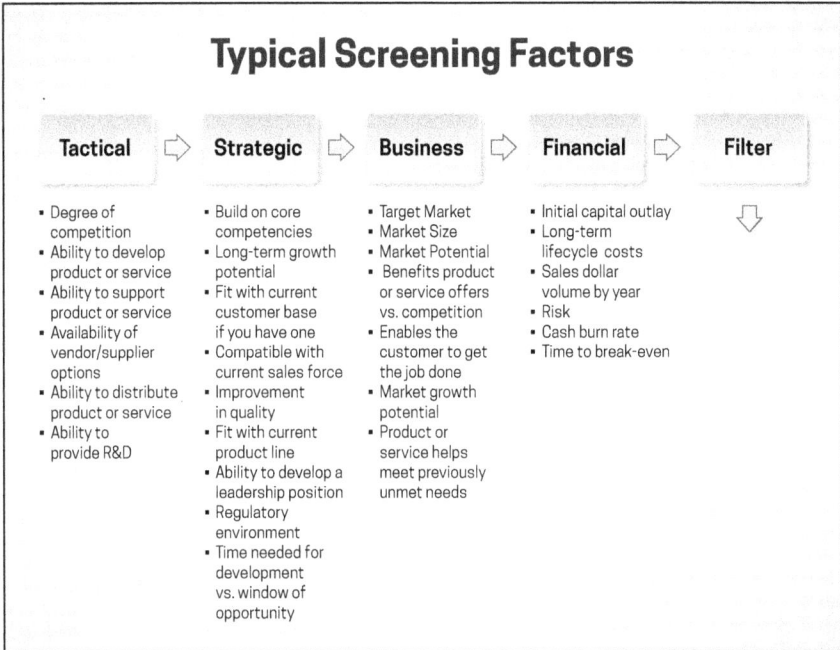

All of these screens can be done by asking several questions related to the idea you are working on. Let's look at each type of screen individually.

Tactical screen elements

For the tactical screen, the questions to ask include:

- How much competition do you see in this market? Is this competition significant or nominal?

- What is your ability to develop this product or service in the market? Can you create it yourself or must it be manufactured?

- How able are you to support your product or service? How much support does it require? Are you able to outsource the necessary support?

- Are vendors readily available?

- How available are suppliers for your product or service? All companies require suppliers. These span the gamut from paper supplies to labor and knowledgeable workers.

- How well can you distribute? Who is incorporated into the distribution channel? How well do you know and understand the distribution channel? Do you have current contacts in this channel?

- What is your ability to perform ongoing product improvement through research and development (R&D)? What will this cost? Must you do this R&D in-house or can you identify an R&D operation with whom you can partner?

- What tactical elements would you add? What screening elements would you use at the sketch phase or at the developmental and exploratory stages? What might you add at the clay model or concept phase? What additional screening elements will be necessary at the prototype stage?

To refer to our travel company example, these groups of proto-ideas and screening elements would include:

Tactical screen elements example

	STRENGTH VS. COMPETITION	ABILITY TO DEVELOP	ABILITY TO SUPPORT	VENDOR AVAILABILITY	YOUR ABILITY TO DISTRIBUTE	ABILITY FOR CONTINUOUS R&D	TOTAL SCORE
	1-10	1-10	1-10	1-10	1-10	1-10	
I wish I could view ancient history	6	10	5	10	5	4	40
I wish my room came with me	Best to combine idea						
How can II develop group vacations for singles	8	10	10	10	8	5	51
How do I take my team on an innovation tour?	10	10	4	8	2	4	38
How do I develop religious travel?	5	10	5	4	4	3	31
I wish I could reward my team	Best to combine idea						
How do I develop specialized school groups, like teams and bands	6	9	9	5	8	7	44
How do I develop tours for teachers?	5	9	9	8	9	7	44
How do I develop a large group vacation and rent a villa?	10	8	9	8	9	5	49
I wish I got college credit for travel	Best to combine idea						
I wish I could go on a foodie tour	10	10	10	7	8	9	54
I wish ocean cruises existed for business	6	7	6	6	7	10	42

Consider your project. What tactical elements would you use in screening? What screening elements would you use at the sketch phase? What elements might you add at the developmental and exploratory stages? What might you add at the clay model or concept phase? What additional screening elements must be added at the prototype stage?

Remember, if you combine ideas, these new ideas need to be rescreened from the beginning.

Strategic screen elements

- Does your offering play off your strengths (knowledge, skills, technical capacity, etc.)?

- What is the long-term growth potential of your offering?

- If you are already in business, does this offering fit your customer base?

- If you have a sales force, is this offering compatible with their skills? If the sales force is new and you need additional sales professionals, are they available?

- Can you build a leadership position that will make you best-in-class?

- If regulations exist, can you meet the rigorous regulatory requirements?

- Is the timing right?

- What strategic elements would you add?

Strategic screen elements example

	CORE COMPETENCIES	LONG-TERM GROWTH POTENTIAL	FIT TO CUSTOMER BASE	SALES FORCE COMPATIBLE	BUILD TO BEST IN CLASS	MEET THE REGULATORY REQUIREMENTS	IS TIMING RIGHT	
	1-10	1-10	1-10	1-10	1-10	1-10	1-10	
I wish I could see ancient history	8	6	7	5	7	10	4	47
I wish my room came with me	Combine idea							
Group vacations for singles	8	10	6	5	8	10	9	56
How to take my team on an innovation tour	6	10	5	4	9	10	8	52
How to develop religious travel…	9	8	8	6	8	10	7	56
I wish I could reward my team	7	8	5	5	8	8	8	49
Specialized school groups, like teams and bands	9	9	7	7	9	7	7	55
Develop tours for teachers	9	7	8	7	8	8	8	55
I wish I could rent a villa	4	4	3	4	3	10	3	31
I wish I got college credit for travel	2	5	7	7	6	3	6	36
I wish I could go on a foodie tour	10	10	8	8	9	10	10	65
I wish ocean cruises existed for business	6	8	5	4	6	10	8	47

Business screen elements

- What is the market potential?

- Does this offering provide significant benefits?

- To what degree does your product or service fulfill unmet needs in the market?

- Do you risk to cannibalizing audience from one of your other products?

- What business elements would you add?

Business screen elements examples

	MARKET POTENTIAL	SIGNIFICANT BENEFITS	DEGREE OF UNMET NEEDS	CANNIBALIZATION OF CURRENT PRODUCTS 10 = LITTLE CANNIBALIZATION 1 = LOTS	
	1-10	1-10	1-10		
I wish I could see ancient history	8	5	4	7	24
I wish my room went with me	Combine idea				
Group vacations for singles	9	8	6	8	31
How to take my team on an innovation tour	5	5	4	10	24
How to develop religious travel...	10	10	7	9	36
I wish I could reward my team	6	9	4	10	29
Specialized school groups, like teams and bands	10	10	7	10	37
Develop tours for teachers	10	10	6	10	36
Large group vacation - rent a villa	7	6	5	7	25
I wish I got college credit for travel	8	9	6	7	30
I wish I could go on a foodie tour	10	10	8	8	36
I wish ocean cruises existed for business	5	4	2	10	21

Financial screening elements

- What is your estimated capital outlay?

- How much sales dollar volume would be generated each year?

- What time will it take to break even?

- What financial elements would you add?

Financial screening elements example

	CAPITAL OUTLAY	SALES VOLUME PER YEAR	TIME TO BREAKEVEN IN YEARS	OTHER
	1-10	1-10		
I wish I could see ancient history	5	4	3-5	
I wish my room went with me		Combine idea		
Group vacations for singles	3	7	2	
How to take my team on an innovation tour	6	3	5	
How to develop religious travel	4	4	5	
I wish I could reward my team	6	3	7	
Specialized school groups, like teams and bands	7	8	5	
Develop tours for teachers	4	8	3	
I wish I could -rent a villa	7	2	7	
I wish I got college credit for travel	4	6	3	
I wish I could go on a foodie tour	6	10	2	
I wish ocean cruises existed for business	7	2	8	

As you continue to work on screening proto-ideas, combine your ideas, create new proto-ideas and research each so they evolve and take shape. They will gradually morph from very rough sketches to more detailed drawings. As these ideas take shape, they will transform into the early stages of the clay model. This process is highly iterative and takes time. As illustrated below, the path on which you now travel has moved. You have passed through the idea generation and screen phases and now will progress to the concept development phase.

Innovation process flow

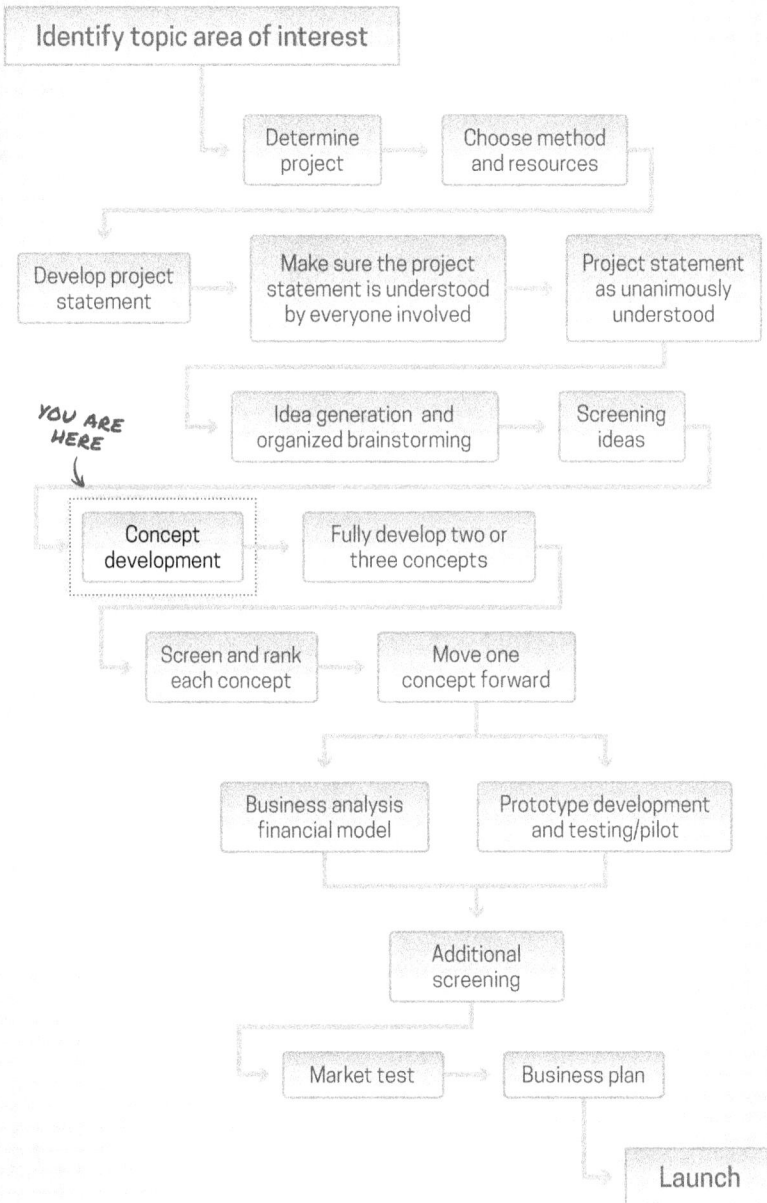

Identify topic area of interest

Determine project

Choose method and resources

Develop project statement

Make sure the project statement is understood by everyone involved

Project statement as unanimously understood

YOU ARE HERE

Idea generation and organized brainstorming

Screening ideas

Concept development

Fully develop two or three concepts

Screen and rank each concept

Move one concept forward

Business analysis financial model

Prototype development and testing/pilot

Additional screening

Market test

Business plan

Launch

The next task is to develop several concept statements using the proto-ideas created. These must be tested and screened. Remember that it is fine to return to the exploratory and development phases as, during testing, you may find that the concepts do not work well. Sometimes project ideas may require starting over from the beginning several times.

Keep in mind that once you enter the concept stage, you must continue to test the concepts against the project statement and the screens you have developed. You also will create more detailed screens as the concepts evolve. The diagram below explains the full progression.

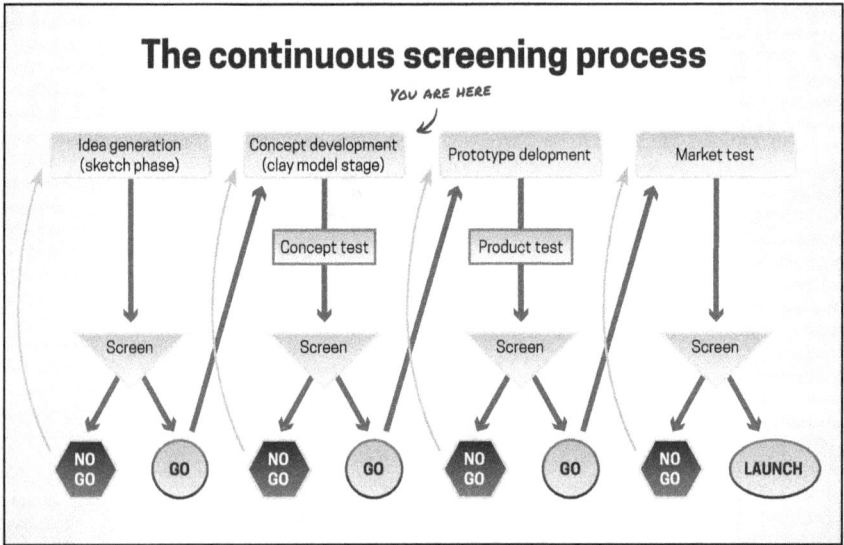

The continuous screening process

YOU ARE HERE

Idea generation (sketch phase)	Concept development (clay model stage)	Prototype delopment	Market test
	Concept test	Product test	
Screen	Screen	Screen	Screen
NO GO / GO	NO GO / GO	NO GO / GO	NO GO / LAUNCH

During the idea and screening phases, resist the temptation to move away from your project statement. Do not take it in a different, completely new direction. Be conscious of your goals and what you hope to accomplish, at all times.

CHAPTER 6

Further analysis and development

"Never leave the egg in you not laid. Don't leave
the laid eggs not hatched. You deserve the best.
You were created to use every gift in you."
~ ISRAELMORE AYIVOR, GHANA AUTHOR

After you screen your ideas, decide how many of them should move
forward for development. Be practical. If you are developing the ideas
on your own, choose only two or three. If you are working with a team,
limit the ideas to between three and five. The next phase involves developing each preliminary concept. In a nutshell, these steps include:

1. Develop each preliminary product concept

2. Identify opportunities that meet customer needs

3. Assess preliminary competitive threats

4. Assess resource requirements

5. Begin the thought process for business case development

6. Screen preliminary concepts and determine closeness of fit to
   your project statement

7. Form a team in order to proceed with this concept

The purpose of this phase is to refine the product or service definition to the point where the concept can be prototyped and evaluated. This helps achieve a more complete understanding of what it will take to fully deploy and assess both the market and financial value of the effort. This will allow you to decide whether to proceed further.

Once you complete this concept stage, the output should be a refined and tested and the concept well defined. This concept evaluation should lead to a decision, and, in some cases, a recommendation to proceed with the design and development of the product or service and begin to commit resources, or to decide not to proceed further.

Once again, remember to review the innovation process flow diagram. If this is a linear process, you now need to decide between screening and/or proto-ideas. Then identify two or three more fully developed concepts, or clay models, to pass through the process. Again, this is a highly iterative process, so you will most likely alternate between explorations of proto-ideas and preliminary concepts as the ideas morph and repeatedly are screened.

For a more in-depth view of this stage, the actual detail flow chart below is one used by a major insurance company and their communications partner. Due to their industry standards and its regulatory environment, as well as the high cost of innovation, the flow chart for this concept phase has many important components.

Innovation process flow

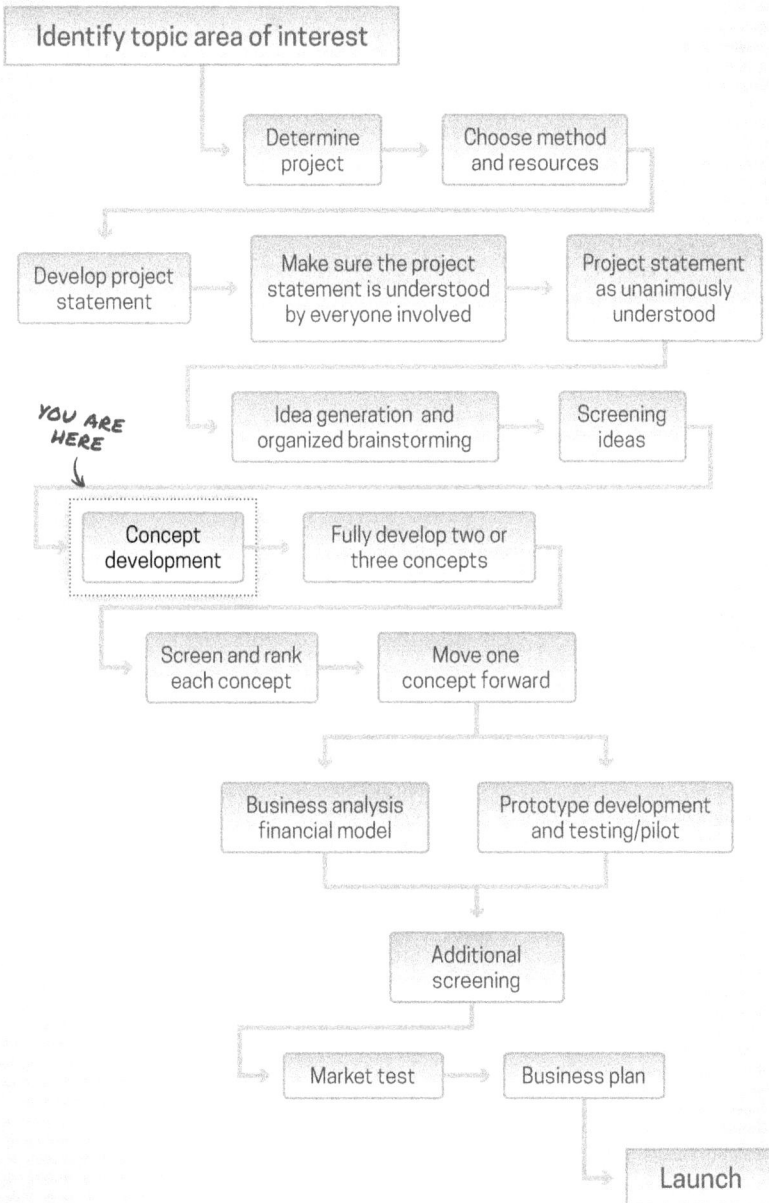

Identify topic area of interest

Determine project

Choose method and resources

Develop project statement

Make sure the project statement is understood by everyone involved

Project statement as unanimously understood

YOU ARE HERE

Idea generation and organized brainstorming

Screening ideas

Concept development

Fully develop two or three concepts

Screen and rank each concept

Move one concept forward

Business analysis financial model

Prototype development and testing/pilot

Additional screening

Market test

Business plan

Launch

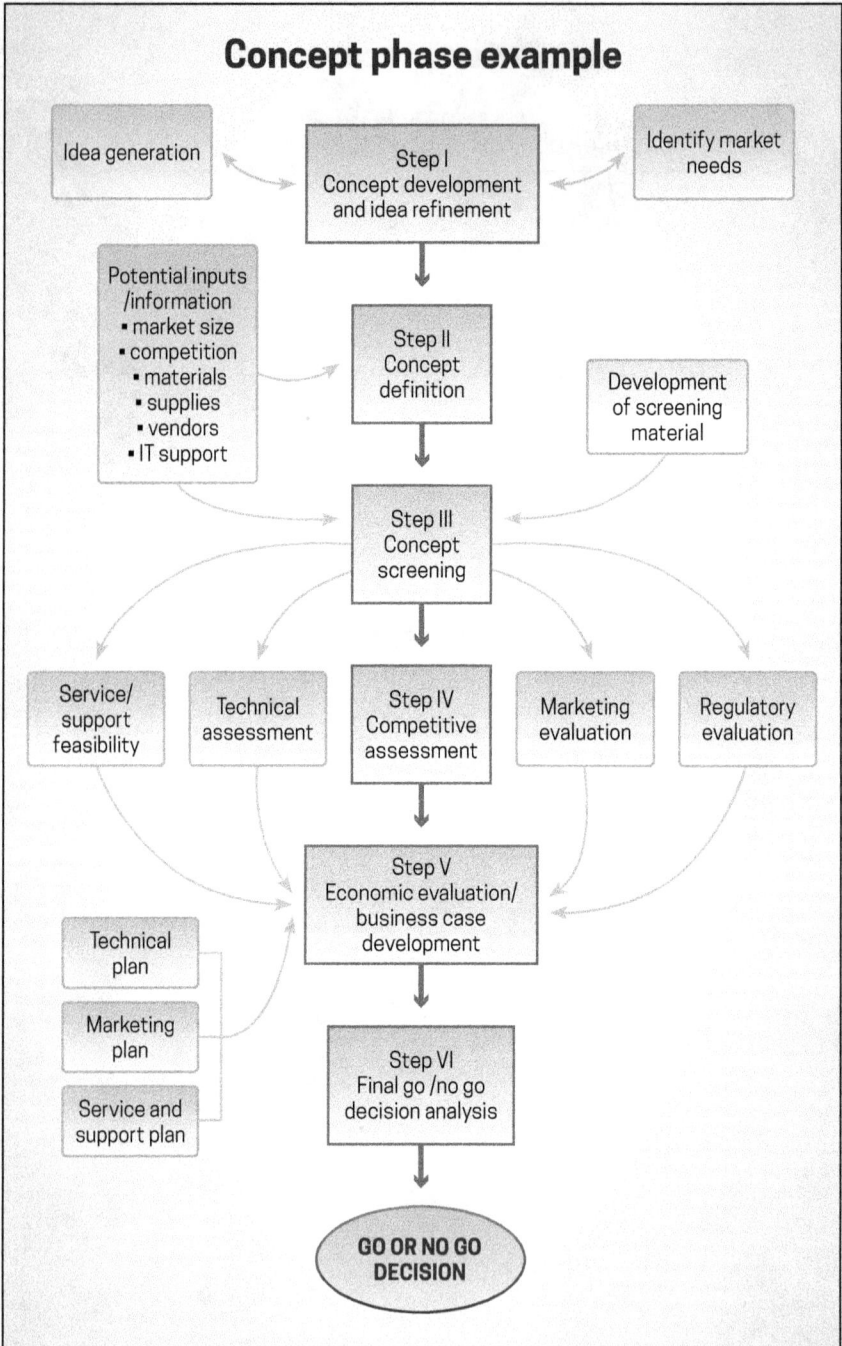

Concept phase example

Idea generation → **Step I** Concept development and idea refinement ← Identify market needs

Potential inputs /information
- market size
- competition
- materials
- supplies
- vendors
- IT support

→ **Step II** Concept definition

Development of screening material

Step III Concept screening

Service/ support feasibility | Technical assessment | **Step IV** Competitive assessment | Marketing evaluation | Regulatory evaluation

Step V Economic evaluation/ business case development

Technical plan

Marketing plan

Service and support plan

Step VI Final go /no go decision analysis

GO OR NO GO DECISION

Despite the circumstance, whether you work on your own, with a small group or in a large company, you will need to spend a period of time to reflect on what elements are necessary for your concept phase and which participants should be involved in the process.

In most cases, with a larger group, it is wise to form a cross-functional team at the beginning of the project in order to take the project from development of the proto-ideas all through to the development of the business plan. One member of this team should continue to lead the project once it is funded. This usually is not an issue for the individual or small firm, as most, if not all of the resources are committed to the project by this time.

Preliminary market concepts

Once some proto-ideas are established, combine and mold them into a preliminary market concept, which should be a concise, initial description of the product or service and should contain the following elements:

(Note: To arrive at the preliminary market concept, I normally expand proto-ideas by putting them into a simple headline format first and then move the ideas into a preliminary market concept. This is how the below elements are structured.)

- **Headline:** Capture the idea in a few words.

- **What is the idea?** Explain the idea with a one or two sentence description.

- **How does this work?** Tell what the idea proposes to accomplish and how it proposes to achieve it within one to three sentences.

- **Who is it for?** In one or two sentences, describe the key constituents who will benefit from the idea.

- **What are the benefits to the user?** Provide a bulleted list of the idea's key strengths and how constituents will benefit from using this product or service.

Here are some examples of more complete vs. incomplete concepts:

MORE COMPLETE	INCOMPLETE
Zap - a sporty version of a subcompact car. Small, light and fast with responsive handling and aggressive design. Sell at an affordable price to the base model	Zap - a transportation machine with a gasoline engine, transmission, front wheel drive and frame. Lots of optional features, plus the latest technology
Nostalgia beer – a double strength beer that recaptures the enjoyment of the 1800s	Nostalgia beer – a beer that tastes great
The Cutter- A fast, good looking haircut for only $10 with no waiting time & services that are always available	The Cutter – A haircut service

Return to the proto-ideas developed for the vacation business in the previous chapter. Review a few of the ideas that passed your screening process and develop headline format sheets like this:

HEADLINE	FOODIE TOUR
What is it?	A tour for individuals who are interested in regional, ethnic and exotic foods from around the world
How does it work?	Set up tours to foreign places to visit restaurants and cooking schools to learn different food preparation techniques.
Who is it for?	Individuals interested in different foods, cultures and food preparation
Benefits to the user?	In-depth study, experiential learning, hands-on experiences with niche experts

HEADLINE	GROUP VACATION FOR SINGLES
What is it?	Destination vacation with lots of activities to promote group participation
How does it work?	Individuals sign up and are matched up by interest, activity level (active vs. passive) and age groupings
Who is it for?	Those who are 21 and older, and single seeking group activities and structure
Benefits to the user?	No hassles, everything included and prearranged, given a fixed price and an opportunity to meet other people, plus the assurance participants will be part of a group and not singled out.

HEADLINE	SPECIALIZED SCHOOL GROUP TRIPS
What is it?	Combination of travel, performance opportunities, exposure to different cultural venues
How does it work?	School bands, sports teams visit international locations and experience the cultural differences, meet individuals from the other cultures with similar interests, and perform with and against other international groups
Who is it for?	Band directors, coaches, students ages 15-24
Benefits to the user?	International experiences, team building, learning at different levels

Here is another one from a different product category to help demonstrate the process.

HEADLINE	THE ZAP
What is it?	Sporty version of a sub-compact car
How does it work?	It is small, light-weight and responsive, contains the latest design elements
Who is it for?	The sports car enthusiast on a budget
Benefits to the user?	Low cost of operation, sporty image, environmentally conscious and responsible

As you can see, the simple proto-ideas have begun to transform from rough sketches into a concept with additional details, even though these details are far from complete. Since the proto-idea has changed, it is now prudent to once again review each headlined proto-idea against the project statement. Once that is done, you may or may not want to modify the headline form to meet the project statement requirements.

The next stop on the road to develop a more complete concept statement is to provide more extensive, complete answers to the following questions. These may require some research. However, you can use the results of this development as a tool to test your potential target market about how well they understand the viability of your product or services. This more specific concept statement also will help you gain valuable feedback to assist the continued evolution of your million-dollar business idea. To gain usable feedback, the concept must be clear and understandable. Answer the following set of questions, then refine them to help develop a solid concept statement:

- **What is your core offering or idea?** This is the base level sometimes known as the core benefit. It is the basic product or service you want the customer to buy. In our Zap example, it is transportation.

- **What does the offering do?** This is a simple description of what the product does. The Zap provides highly stylish transportation at a low cost.

- **How does the offering work? What are the Zap's functions and mechanisms?** This lightweight automobile has a four-cylinder engine and a six-speed transmission.

- **What does the product look like?** This question is not about just the physical appearance, but also may be a description of the product or service provided. The Zap is a sporty model of an economy car.

- **What are its components?** For the vacation examples, this could be housing, transportation, events and much more. For the Zap it is the frame, drive train, engine, tires, and fuel tank.

- **What is your tangible offering?** This will turn the core offering or benefit into a basic product customers would require. For the Zap, a customer would count on the vehicle to have a transmission, a body, wheels, seats and other key parts, and provide reliable transportation.

- **What is your augmented offer?** This would detail additional benefits and features that differentiate this product or service from the competition and make it desirable. For the car example, this would be its European handling, the fact the car is fitted with the latest technology, and that it comes complete with GPS integrated Wi-Fi, voice commands and auto-parking capabilities.

- **What benefits - or product or service strength - does this provide the customer?** Product benefits are the cornerstone of your of product or service planning. These key benefits assist with the psychological positioning of this product against the competition and fulfill the product or service promises. A well-developed benefit proposition statement should be clear, concise and direct. Also, the statement must address the crucial characteristics of the product or service. Example: Floating Ivory soap for bubble baths eliminates any need to slip around and look for soap while in the tub.

- **Who are your prospects?** The first task is to find prospects that will benefit from the product. In our prior Zap car example, individuals concerned about owning a low cost vehicle with, a sporty image and who are concerned about environmental friendliness should be on that prospect list. Many factors can be used to identify these prospects based on the benefits offered. Some factors to keep in mind are demographics, behavioral patterns and psychographics.

- **What do your prospects look like?** What is their psycho demographic profile? Once again, examples from the Zap instance might be their value orientation, their desire to care for the environment, or their self-esteem or self-image.

- **What are your customer's unique needs?** Example: Does the customer want or need to be frugal? Zap offers a sporty car to those on a tight budget.

- **What is your value proposition?** Remember, the value proposition solves a customer problem or satisfies a customer needs. The value proposition may consist of a bundle of products and services that meet the requirements of only a specific customer segment. Example: This sports car offers outstanding design, excellent handling and is priced for the budget conscience.

- **Who is the competition?** List both your direct and indirect competitors.

- **What are the product or service price, promotion and distribution strategies?** What product or service currently exists as the price leader? Is there price discrimination within a market? What are the list pricing, discounts, allowances and payment periods or credit terms? The possibilities abound, however, what does the particular market segment addressed by this product or service expect?

- **What types of promotion will be used?** Consider all available tools, including sales promotions, advertising, sales force, Internet, e-marketing (website, Facebook, Twitter, Instagram, LinkedIn, and eBay to name just a few), public relations, e-marketing and direct marketing (telemarketing, billboards).

- **How will the product or service be distributed?** Will you use direct distribution or use intermediaries? If you plan to use intermediaries, which and how many will you use? Will you use intensive, selective, or exclusive distribution?

Consider these important points as you begin to develop your complete concept statement, or clay model, for concept development:

- Keep your concept(s) to stay as single-minded, focused, direct and concise as possible.

- Considering both perceived and real benefits, keep in mind what makes your concept unique. Identify your specific advantage over the competition.

- Avoid limiting creativity. You will screen and prioritize your ideas later in the process.

- Rather than narrowing your concepts too quickly consider all possible target audiences and benefits. Do not over- or underestimate the competition.

To assist you with your total market concept development, the necessary forms are provided in Appendix C. These will help you identify study, discuss and clarify your ideas, as well as build them into a total market concept.

For demonstration purposes, the grid below shows one of the beginning concepts. If you explore this, along with the three or four other concepts you want to advance, use the concept forms provided in Appendix C to develop them. Do not skip any steps, but do review the project statement again before you begin. Here is the concept to develop into the clay model:

HEADLINE	FOODIE TOUR
What is it?	A tour for individuals interested in various regional, ethnic and exotic foods throughout the world
How does it work?	The tour will visit foreign (or exotic?) restaurants and cooking schools in other parts of the world in order to sample a variety of foods, as well as learn different food preparation techniques.
Who is it for?	Individuals interested in different foods, cultures and food preparation
Benefits to the user?	In-depth study, learn experientially with hands-on experiences provided by experts

Spend some time to review the incomplete concept statement before you begin to do more research on what exists in the marketplace. Navigate the Internet on the computer, but spend no more then thirty minutes to an hour performing very basic research. During this initial research period, look for offerings currently in the marketplace. What makes your offering different? How can you modify or improve your offering to make it even more attractive?

Once you do this research, it is time to begin to construct the complete concept statement. Develop this concept statement by answering the questions on the Total Concept Definition worksheet forms found in Appendix C. If you working with a team, you may want to divide the team and distribute one concept to each division of the group. Then each group would move the concept forward toward the completion stage. If you work alone, tackle only one concept at a time and and focus on each individually until all are completed.

As you develop each concept, continue to brainstorm and adjust each, as this process is still very interactive. Know that it is common to review each concept, question by question, a number of times. As each answer changes, it is most likely the others will change as well. This means your basic idea will progress gradually from pencil sketch ➜ rough clay model ➜ clay model.

The following is an expanded concept statement for the Foodie Tour:

Total concept definition worksheet culinary travel
Core idea definition and development

WHAT IS THE CORE IDEA?	Culinary travel
WHAT DOES IT DO?	Provides unique and memorable culinary experiences of all kinds
HOW DOES IT WORK?	Travel to a region and experience in-depth, guided exposure to the local cuisine and culture. The experience takes place within small groups of no larger then twenty individuals.
WHAT DOES IT LOOK LIKE?	Experience local and regional restaurants, food markets, farm stands, farms, wineries, dairies, commercial kitchens, and cooking classes taught by the pros
WHAT ARE THE COMPONENTS?	Transportation, hotels, professional guides, classes, and cultural experiences
WHAT ARE THE BENEFITS?	Adventure, relaxation, education, culture, history, as well as hands-on learning about local foods and food preparation

Total concept definition worksheet culinary travel

Product / service offering and target prospects

WHAT IS THE CORE OFFERING ?	Augmented offering
WHAT IS THE TANGIBLE OFFERING?	Personal indulgence · Tangible offering · Romance · Eating · Tours · Core offering · Culinary travel · Nutrition · Learning
WHAT IS THE AUGMENTED OFFERING?	The good life · Nightlife

WHO ARE THE PROSPECTS?	Target segment 1 **Explores**	Target Segment 2 **Food Enthusiasts**	Target Segment 3 **Cultural Tourists**
WHAT ARE THEIR UNIQUE NEEDS?	• Seeking new cuisine • Learning food preparation • Experience local culture • Have unique dinning experience	• Learn food preparation • Work with expert • Hands on experience • Work with fresh local ingredients	• Unique meals • Local restaurants • Good wine and specialty food • Romance
WHAT DO THE PROSPECTS LOOK LIKE?	• Foodie adventure seeker • Fun open minded • Between 18 and 95 • Healthy • Thirsting for life adventures	• Cooking for a hobby • Seeking new recipes and preparation techniques • Between 18 and 95	• Thirsting for the adventure of life through food and culture

Total concept definition worksheet culinary travel
Who is the competition?

WHAT IS THE VALUE PROPOSITION?		Segment I Explores	Segment II Food Enthusiasts	Segment III Cultural Tourist
	What are the segment's Value-added offerings?	• Local cuisine • Adventurous food • Small classes	• Learn from local chefs • Use local ingredients	• Excellent dining • Relaxed atmosphere
	What is the core offering?	• Culinary travel, learning about food types and how to prepare national and regional cuisine		

WHO IS THE COMPETITION?	
	Competitor 1 Trafalgar
	Competitor 2 Culinary Travel Corporation
	Competitor 3 All Travel
	(Other potential competitors: Wine Tours International, and self-guided tours)

Total concept definition worksheet culinary travel
Beginning business case definitions

PRODUCT	National and international culinary travel
PRICE	$2,000 per person and up
DISTRIBUTION	• Travel agents • Association groups
PROMOTION	• Travel agent shows • Websites\social media • Trade publications • Direct sales force
REGULATIONS	Unknown

Once the concept statement seems somewhat solid, perform the following exercise to determine the group's true feelings and thoughts about this concept. Ask the following questions in this sequence:

- What are the positives of this concept?

- How can this concept be improved?

- For each of these questions, cultivate a potential list of suggestions for how to improve each concept at each point.

Once this exercise is complete, you may or may not change the concept statement. If changes are made, as always, make sure they align with the project statement requirements. Always rescreen the concept to ensure it continues to meet the criteria. This might sound reptitive, but it is very easy to become sidetracked by minor tweaks that are off target.

The next step is to build your "storyboard.". Storyboards are used by movie and TV producers, new product/service developers, advertisers, and scriptwriters to combine pictures with text to bring a concept into focus so it can be tested and refined.. Storyboarding alone will not make you expert; some researchers say that to become an expert in a topic or a skill takes thousands of hours of pratice and study. storyboarding will provide you with much of the information necessary to prepare and create a more complete concept. .Try this exercise to gain some hands-on experience in developing and working with a total market concept. It could prove both fun and helpful. The Orange exercise, contained in Appendix D, was developed by Michael Krauss and used very succesfully to help individuals better understand the use of the total market concept. Below are some necessary tools and simple instructions:

- You will need copies of the total market definition worksheets one through five, found in Appendix C, plus the answer sheet to the Orange exercise, found in Appendix D.

- If this is a group project, divide into smaller groups of four or five.

- If this is a solo project, you are ready to go.

- You will need one orange for each person in your group.

- Tell each person that they must suspend all beliefs.

The directions:

Your company research and development department just developed a new food product, never before experienced by anyone in the world. It is a unique combination of citric acid, a peel and a flavor. Some early prototypes will have seeds while others will not. Some contain more juice, while others will be engineered with a more meaty texture. We will name it an "orange!"

Your task is to use the orange as a possible new food product and develop the total concept statement. Follow the process explained in this chapter. At the end of this exercise, explain the pros, the cons, and a list of suggested improvements for the "orange."

Upon the completion of this "Orange" exercise, return to the foodie concept, which now has the working title of "Culinary." Next, develop a storyboard for testing this concept with the potential target audience. To do that, you must develop a storyboard for each concept. Each storyboard consists of a short narrative or a narrative combined with a drawing or photograph. Create a handout as well. This handout will contain the same narrative and drawing, accompanied by questions about the likelihood people will purchase this product. Present the concept storyboards and narratives to a group of eight people. Each group participant will also complete the handout, selecting only one of the following choices:

- I would definitely buy.

- I would probably buy.

- I might or might not buy.

- I would probably not buy.

- I would definitely not buy.

Collect these forms from each participant as he or she leaves the session.

If two-thirds of the respondents check either "Iwould definitely buy" or "I would probably buy," you may have a good concept. Any result less than two-thirds agreement and you need to revisit this concept. Gather feedback, then rework and retest the concept. "How to test these concepts" will be explained in more depth in the next chapter.

After you develop the storyboard or narrative, return to the concept form that identified prospective clients. In the case of the Culinary Travel example, the three prospects identified were explorers, food enthusiasts and cultural tourists. Create a storyboard for each of these three prospects. When you do, tailor the narative, as well as the graphic you choose, to each of the prospect groups. Keep the narrative concise, as shown below, in order to test your assumptions.

The following examples of storyboards were drawn based on the Culinary Travel concept forms:

STORYBOARD   **The Food Enthusiasts**

Travel nationally and internationally with a small group of fellow food enthusiasts to experience regional cuisine. Learn from local chefs and experience hands-on preparation and cooking techniques for local dishes.

Experience local culture and customs.

The Food Enthusiasts' tour handles all transportation and accommodations for a fixed price of between $2k to $9k.

Photographs in these storyboards are licensed from istockphoto.com

The following handhout examples were drawn from the Culinary Travel concept form:

The Food Enthusiasts

Travel nationally and internationally with a small group of fellow food enthusiasts to experience regional cuisine. Learn from local chefs and experience hands-on preparation and cooking techniques for local dishes.

Experience local culture and customs.

The Food Enthusiasts' tour handles all transportation and accommodations for a fixed price of between $2k to $9k.

How interested would you be in purchasing the vacation package described above if it were available to you?

- ❏ I would definitely buy
- ❏ I would probably buy
- ❏ I might or might not buy
- ❏ I would probably not buy
- ❏ I would definitely not buy

Photographs in these storyboards are licensed from istockphoto.com

Storyboard and handout for Explorer's Concept Statement

Explorer's Tour

Travel nationally and internationally with a small group of fellow food enthusiasts to experience regional cuisine. Learn from local chefs and experience hands-on preparation and cooking techniques for local dishes.

Experience local culture and customs.

The Food Enthusiasts' tour handles all transportation and accommodations for a fixed price of between $2k to $9k.

Photographs in these storyboards are licensed from istockphoto.com

Explorer's Tour

Travel nationally and internationally with a small group of fellow food enthusiasts to experience regional cuisine, learn from local chefs and experience hands - on preparation and cooking of local dishes.

Experience local culture and customs.

The Food Enthusiasts' tour handles all transportation and accommodations for a fixed price of between $2k to $9k.

How interested would you be in purchasing the vacation package described above if it were available to you?

❑ I would definitely buy
❑ I would probably buy
❑ I might or might not buy
❑ I would probably not buy
❑ I would definitely not buy

Photographs in the storyboards are licensed from istockphoto.com

Storyboard and Handout
for the Cultural Tourist Concept

STORYBOARD

Cultural Tourist

Travel nationally and internationally with a small group of fellow food enthusiasts to experience regional cuisine. Learn from local chefs and experience hands-on preparation as well as the cooking techniques for local dishes.

Experience local culture and customs.

The Food Enthusiasts' tour handles all transportation and accommodations for a fixed price of between $2k to $9k.

The photographs in these storyboards are licensed from istockphoto.com

HANDOUT	**Cultural Tourist**

Travel nationally and internationally with a small group of fellow food enthusiasts to experience regional cuisine. Learn from local chefs and experience hands-on preparation as well as cooking techniques for local dishes.

Experience local culture and customs.

The Food Enthusiasts' tour handles all transportation and accommodations for a fixed price of between $2k to $9k.

How interested would you be in purchasing the vacation package described above if it were available to you?

❏ I would definitely buy
❏ I would probably buy
❏ I might or might not buy
❏ I would probably not buy
❏ I would definitely not buy

Photographs in the storyboards are licensed from istockphoto.com

Hopefully, you are working on your own project as these book chapters progress. If so, it is time to create your own concept statements. Follow the flow of this chapter, and, at the end of the process, you will have storyboards and handouts to illustrate your own concepts targeted toward your specific potential prospects.

The next chapter will guide you on the path to research and test your concepts.

Take a moment to review. Where are you on this journey? Hopefully, you are not discouraged. You learned in chapter one that, as an entrepreneur, you will travel along a road filled with tasks and tests. Along this road filled with trials, each test and task will need to be addressed as they present themselves. In most cases, each must be successfully tackled. This requires persistence and determination. If you feel knocked down, get up and begin again. Be flexible and work hard, but also work smart.

Remember, this is a time of transformation. Obstacles and discoveries appear at practically every stage; these can be difficult to overcome. From personal experience, one instance occurred when we just completed what we believed was a winning concept. We built the storyboards, developed a presentation for a client and felt amazing. The morning of our client presentation arrived. Just as we were about to go inside, we heard a radio commercial from one of our client's main competitors. This commercial announced their new product – a product almost identical to the one we were about to present to this client. To overcome what could have been a devastating blow, we dusted ourselves off and pulled out our other concepts. Having developed multiple concepts and storyboards proved beneficial. Plan B quickly became Plan A.

C H A P T E R   7

Refining your concept

*"The process and organization leading up to cooking
the egg can tell you a lot about the cook."*
~ DAVID CHANG

You now have developed some concepts to be tested, and you have your storyboards available. Now what? Now is the time to refine your concept. Below are some questions to consider about assessing opportunities.

- What is an opportunity assessment?

- Who is the target market?

- What types of market research I need to do?

- How attractive is the market?

- What is the opportunity?

- How attractive is the opportunity?

- How do I test the concepts?

- What are the research methods?

- How do I prepare to do the research?

Innovation process flow

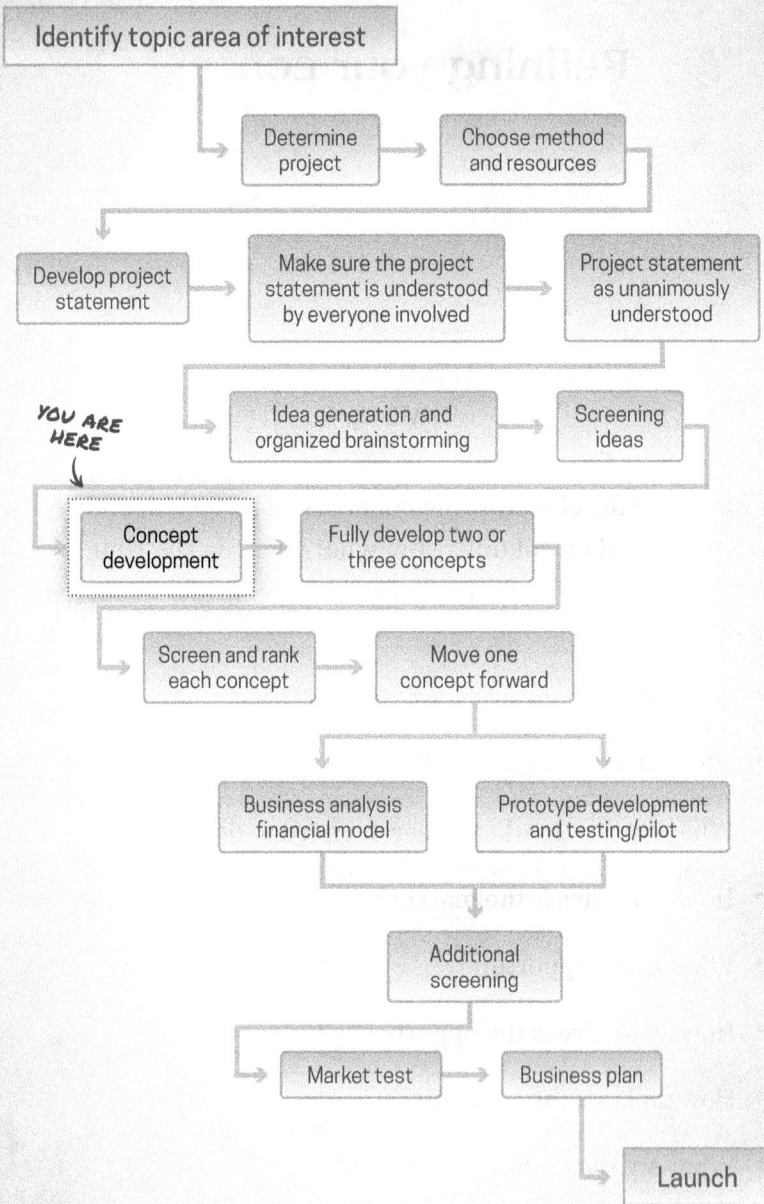

Identify topic area of interest

Determine project

Choose method and resources

Develop project statement

Make sure the project statement is understood by everyone involved

Project statement as unanimously understood

Idea generation and organized brainstorming

Screening ideas

YOU ARE HERE

Concept development

Fully develop two or three concepts

Screen and rank each concept

Move one concept forward

Business analysis financial model

Prototype development and testing/pilot

Additional screening

Market test

Business plan

Launch

- What do I want to learn from the concept testing?

- How do I develop a discussion guide for my project?

  Note: the terms "discussion guide" and "script" will be used interchangeably

- How do I run a group session for my project?

- How do I collect data for my project?

- What do I do I have the data for my project?

Until now you have done only minor research, which resulted in concepts developed from the current knowledge obtained by you and your team. This will color how you view the world, how your mind edits reality. If you are working with a team within a corporate culture, this could add another set of lenses through which your worldview is filtered. Now it is the time to expand the limits past the initial impressions your team originally held. You can now perform tests outside the confinements of your space.

Market research includes both qualitative and quantitative tools and techniques. Included are only a few of the vast array of tools available to provide at least a basic knowledge of what is available. Many good books are available on this subject if you want to learn more. As we continue along this path through the concept-testing phase, you will focus mostly on qualitative research to explore and clarify concepts.

Marketing research quickly can become both very technical and very expensive. The goal is to provide the entrepreneur and the small businessperson with basic tools to advance their concept. If adequate funding is available, by all means hire professionals for each phase of the research process, as this will serve you well. However, even if you hire professionals, know what you hope to gain from that research. Consistently ask, "What do I want to know?"

One of the most fascinating products in the world is laundry detergent. Why is it fascinating? Because people tend to base its effectiveness on how well it suds, or foams up when used. The purpose of soap is to loosen dirt from clothing or dishes or our bodies. But soap manufacturers have learned that people will put too much soap in their washer or dishwasher if they don't see enough soap suds. The product doesn't need suds to clean, but people expect it, and depend on the visual action of the soap, rather than the cleanliness of the product to determine the effectiveness.

This leads to problems in determining the right kind and level of chemicals to add to affect the right sudsiness without affecting the cleaning properties. But what it also shows us is that "What do I want to know?" doesn't always give us the answer we're expecting. When you ask someone, "What do you want your laundry detergent or soap to do?" they're most likely to respond, "Get my clothes clean, or get my hair, car, whatever clean." The question you want to ask after that is, "How do you know your clothes are clean? What tells you they're clean?"

When you ask yourself, "Why do I want to know?" also ask yourself, "How will I know I have the answers I need?"

Below are some important terms to understand, along with their definitions. These terms will be used throughout this chapter:

- **Qualitative research** - This is research designed primarily to explore and understand customer activity and feelings to help clarify the concept(s). A good example of qualitative research would be individual and group interviews, such as focus groups.

- **Quantitative research** - This research deals with the numbers and determines the amounts, or proportions of segments of a market, a product or a service.

- **Central location or mall intercept interviews** - These are individual interviews conducted in high traffic areas.

- **In-depth interviews** - These interviews are used to understand what motivates consumer behavior. This kind of interview is similar to the client interview done by a clinical psychologist. It is unstructured and asks many probing questions. This type of research is best done by a professional.

- **Sales force and technical studies** - These analyze sales reports, personal observations, customer letters, emails, and conversations with customers, and customer surveys. It is helpful to ensure the questions asked are uniform. Questions asked in slightly differently ways yield different answers, which will make reliable data analysis difficult. Observations made by the sales or technical support person also should be recorded using a uniform answer sheet.

- **User attitude studies** - These studies gathers information on individuals to see how they structure their perception of their reality and how that perception influences their response to it. Attitude studies usually have a number of components: a cognitive/knowledge component, an affective or liking component, and an intention or action component.

- **Needs or benefit-based segmentation studies** - These studies provide information concerning customer needs, which helps the researcher understand the motivation that directs the consumer toward a goal. For your new business idea, you will look for an unfulfilled need or needs that exist(s) in the market place. Benefit segmentation looks for a segment of the population that would benefit from the product or service being offered.

- **Advance analytical techniques** - These techniques include factor analysis, multidimensional scaling, cluster analysis, conjoint analysis, regression models, and multiple regression models.

Explanation of Terms:

Factor analysis is a statistical method used for trying to discover a few basic factors, which clarify the connection between variables. For example factor analysis can be used to determine underlying attitudes towards types of food products.

Multidimensional scaling is used in marketing for analyzing the preferences and perceptions of respondents. The output is a visual grid known as a perceptional map.

Cluster analysis is used in marketing by placing individuals or objects into mutually exclusive groups. Each group internally should be as much alike as possible and as dissimilar in relation to other groups as possible.

Conjoint analysis is used in marketing to determine the value consumers place on different attributes of the same product.

Regression and multiregression are statistical tools to help estimate the relationship between variables. Regression analysis refers to one dependent variable while multiregression refers to one dependent variable and a number of independent variables. For example, a dependent variable is the price of an item, independent variables would be factors which impact the price such as size, quality, and location to just name a few possibilities. Adding or subtracting independent variables in the analysis of a product will indicate which independent variables add or take away from the product's price. Regression tools also may help determine which of the variables have the most value to a product or service.

Once your concept is developed to the clay model stage, you must research four major areas: **opportunity assessment, market attractiveness, buyer needs**, and **concept testing**. Herein lies a chicken and egg problem. Which do you do first? It doesn't usually matter. The most important thing to do now is to just pick one of the areas and start your work.

1. Opportunity Assessment

Opportunity assessment focuses on the ability to identify the zone of opportunity. To accomplish this, you must understand how the external market intersects with competitive trends and impacts the ability your ability to deliver your product or service. In addition, the entrepreneur must understand the buyer's needs and wants. The one area, which is overlapped by all three of these elements, is your zone of opportunity.

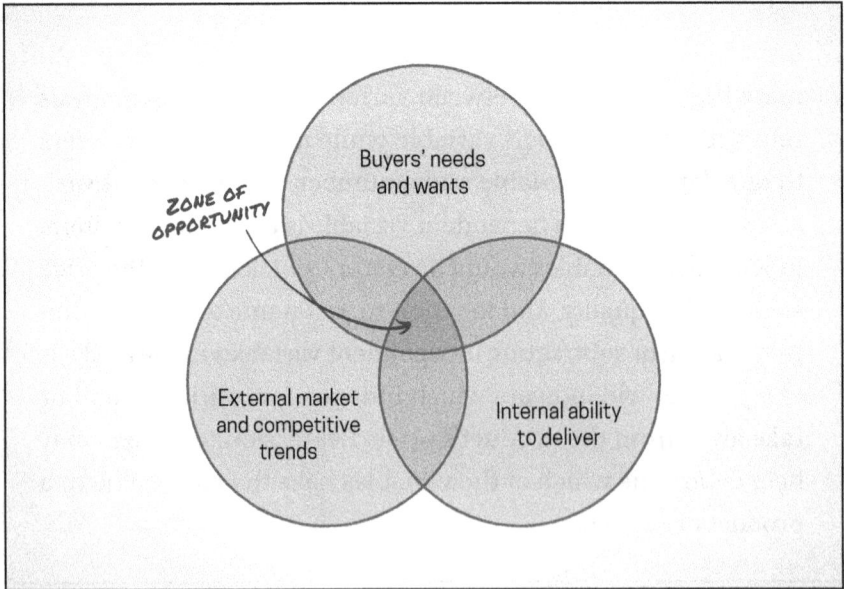

ZONE OF OPPORTUNITY

Buyers' needs and wants

External market and competitive trends

Internal ability to deliver

The zone of opportunity can be identified through important information gathered via a number of channels. One of these channels is to talk with existing customers, if customers exist; this is always a good start. If you currently have no customers, talk to customers who use a similar product or service provided by a potential competitor.

Thought leaders are another great source of information. Check out blogs, discussion groups, the technology, entertainment and design website (www.TED.com), as well as TED speakers, magazine articles, newspapers, and think tanks (which offer a great deal of valuable information on their websites, recorded interviews, online discussions groups, trade publications and websites), just to name a few resources.

Competitive assessments also can be helpful in finding your zone of opportunity. Check publically available sources; perform Internet searches; and search 10K reports, an annual report required by the U.S. Security and Exchange Commission (SEC) for companies with over a specific dollar amount of assets and equity held by 500 or owners. These reports are filed with the Federal Government by appropriate companies. Review potential competitor websites to determine their reputation in the marketplace. Once this important information is gathered, do a mini-SWOT (strength, weakness, opportunity and threat) analysis on each potential competitor.

Remember the discussion of concept development forms in the last chapter? One of the questions was, "Who is the competition?" The form below can be a valuable tool to begin employ as you to investigate potential competitors. Here is the culinary travel example form:

Total concept definition worksheet – The Orange
Who is the competition?

WHAT IS THE VALUE PROPOSITION?		Segment I Shipped fruit	Segment II At-home consumer	Segment III Juice producers
	What are the segment's Value-added offerings?	• Large size • Extra fancy • Sweetest taste	• Refreshing • Satisfies thirst • Nutritious	• Ample supply available on demand
	What is the core offering?	• Fresh • Sweet tasting • Uncontaminated • Consistent taste		
WHO IS THE COMPETITION?	Competitor 1 Other citrus fruits			
	Competitor 2 Breakfast cereals			
	Competitor 3 Vegetable snacks			
	(Other competitors: Vitamins, snack food products, decorative accessories and garnishes)			

The third part of this phase will help determine your ability to deliver on the value proposition.

2. Market Attractiveness

In the earlier chapters, we discussed how to create different types of screens. These screens should have helped you develop questions and criteria for each concept you needed to evaluate. These screens contained a tactical element, a strategic element and a business element, as well as other components. To help you understand market attractiveness, use the market attractiveness matrix.

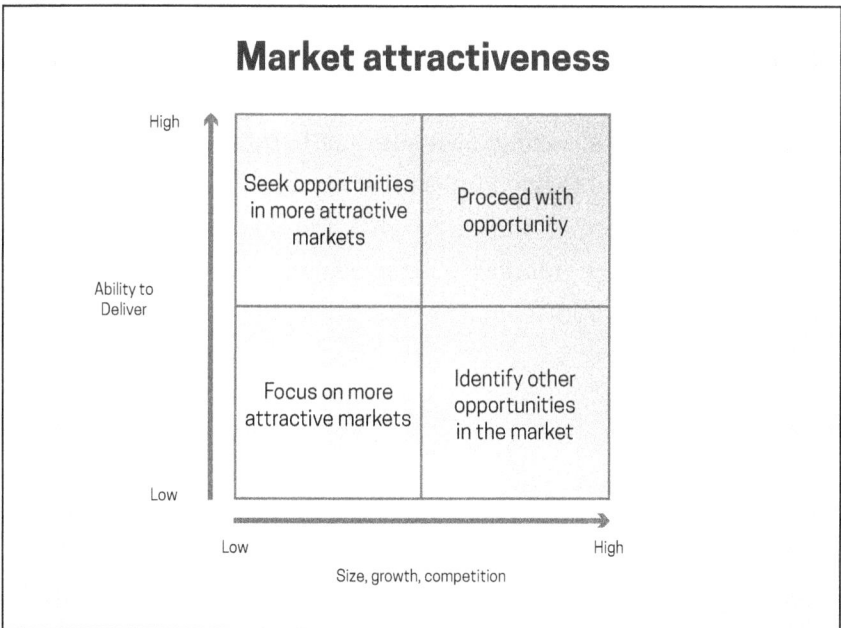

Market attractiveness

High ↑

Ability to Deliver	Seek opportunities in more attractive markets	Proceed with opportunity
	Focus on more attractive markets	Identify other opportunities in the market

Low

Low → High

Size, growth, competition

To help you take full advantage of the market attractiveness matrix, refer back to the screens discussed in chapter five. Elements in your tactical screen can help determine your ability to deliver.

The tactical screen elements include the degree of competition in the market, the ability to develop the market, the ability to produce the product or service; the ability to support the product or service; the availability of vendor supplier options; the ability to distribute; and the ability for continuous improvement, research and development, to name a few.

The strategic screen should question if the concept matches your core competencies, the concept's long-term growth potential and its fit with your customer base. It also illustrates if the concept is compatible with the existing sales force, if it fits with product lines, and its ability to develop into a leadership position, among other necessary questions.

Finally, the business screen asks questions along the line of market potential and target market. These questions include enumerating the product benefits, asking if the product helps the customer to do whatever is required to accomplish the job, and if the product meets needs otherwise unmet. Based on what you discovered these using these three elements - tactical, strategic and business, you should be able to establish a valid estimate of market attractiveness.

3. Buyers' Needs Research

In this chapter we will more closely examine the tools necessary to move your project ahead using buyers needs research, introduced chapter three.

Understanding a buyer's needs is critical to business success. Buyers' needs research can be broken down into two phases – the qualitative and the quantitative.

The qualitative phase encompasses six steps, as illustrated below:

Steps in Buyer Needs Research
QUALITATIVE PHASE

Prepare concept statement

Choose presentation style:
- Narrative
- Drawings
- Prototype

Decide what to communicate

Define respondent group

Early adaptors?
Users?
Demographics?

Select respondent situation

Face-to-face
Mail
Internet

One-on-one
Group

Prepare interviews

Choose content
Avoid bias

Conduct interviews group and individual

Moderate clearly without bias

Use a third party, if possible

Tabulate and analyze results

Analysis is best done within a group

Proceed back to brainstorming development stage
or
Cease exploration and development

The quantitative phase of buyers' needs research includes seven steps:

Steps in Buyer Needs Research
QUANTITATIVE PHASE

Needs definition

Refine statement of need

Define information objective

Determine and define what you want to quantify

Establish research design

Determine who is to be interviewed

Define scope or extent of research

Create survey instrument

Draft questionnaire to elicit feed back on needs

Consumer research

Hire vendor or do it yourself

Screen potential interviewees

Collect data

Tabulate and analyze results

Proceed to quantify need
or
Return to brainstorming
or
Refine hypothetical need and retest
or
Cease exploration in the area

Go or no go decision

Proceed back to brainstorming development stage
or
Cease exploration and development

Below are some of the pros and cons of qualitative research:

Pros – This kind of research:

- Helps to identify basic core needs

- Ensures that you are in touch with the customer at the base level

- Provides additional information, knowledge and experience for continued brainstorming, concept development and product development

- Enables identification of dead-end projects early in the process to conserve resources

- Provides the quantitative foundation for a million dollar idea

Cons – This kind of research:

- Can be a time-consuming and expensive process

- Often appears to be intangible, particularly if you have a bottom line mentality

- Results can be ambiguous and unclear

4. Concept Testing

The objective of a concept test is to discover whether or not the concept is worth pursuing. Is it a strong or weak concept? This testing crudely estimates the sales or trials the service would provide, while it also offers feedback and guidance about how this concept can be improved and modified. It also helps determine if you or your firm has the credibility to provide this product or service, as well as insights into what customers think about alternate products or services. Be aware also that sometimes the product is great, but the packaging is a deterrent. Mothers with small children for instance, prefer to have snacks and treats that their toddler can either open themselves (Juice boxes for instance) or that they can quickly and easily open for them. When testing a concept, test all aspects of the concept, including: size, smell, packaging, ease of storage and other factors.

To gather this information, you will need your concept statement storyboards, a discussion guide and a preselected respondent or respondent group. Questions to keep in mind include:

- How will you approach the respondents? Will you conduct one-on-one interviews or focus groups?

- What demographics will your respondents represent?

- What questions should be asked?

- How many concepts will you reveal? **Note:** It is best to disclose no more than three at a time.

Questions asked may include:

- What do you like about this concept?

- What draws you to this concept?

- What don't you like about this concept?

- What turns you off to this concept?

- What is confusing or incomplete about this concept?

- What additions and/or changes might you make to this concept?

To assess additional information on attitudes, interests, and the probability of purchase, you may ask participants if they definitely would buy; probably would buy; might or might not buy; probably would not buy; or definitely would not buy. From the development of concepts mentioned in chapter six, this is an example of the concept statement and the accompanying questions.

Below is a breakout of the six main steps involved in the research area of concept testing:

Step 1: Prepare your concept statement.

In the first round of preparation, it is best to present a narrative or drawing. Prototypes can prove very expensive and usually are held for the last round of testing. For one client, we set up a live assessment at an airport gate to test a prototype of a specific type of bar code technology for frequent flyers. Without considering the staged portions, which did not work as planned, just the test alone ran between $3,000 and $5,000. This is not what most people would consider pocket change. The cost was unduly expensive for one test.

The narrative, picture, or a combination of both is extremely important. If respondents do not understand your concept, you have wasted both time and money on the test. To ensure the clarity of the intent of any narrative or picture represented, it is best to do a quick test enlisting the opinion of someone totally unfamiliar with the project and the concept. Often, using a friend who will be honest with you is best. However, be certain that person will not disclose the concept tested. It may be prudent to have the selected person sign a nondisclosure agreement (NDA).

Step 2: Define the respondent group(s)

Posing the greatest challenge to any type of marketing research, you must answer three basic questions in order to choose the pool of respondents: Who? How many? How?

The question of **who** enables you to define the target consumer as closely as possible. In our culinary travel concept example, the segment might contain some of these demographic characteristics: individuals have taken group tour vacations, are empty nesters, are middle income young singles, or are small-town executives.

To determining **how many** requires asking a number of associated questions. These include the variance of the population, the magnitude of acceptable error and the confidence level. Each plays an important role in determining the sample size. A small sample size is less reliable, while larger sample sizes are more reliable, therefore it is better to sample a greater number. That said, a good sample can be obtained from less than one percent of the population providing that the correct sampling procedure is used.

Two methods exist for picking the pool: probability and non-probability. Probability consists of simple random samples, stratified random samples (samples drawn from within a band that are equal on some attribute), and cluster samples. The probability method tends to be expensive and time-consuming to execute.

For our purposes, we will work with the non-probability method, which includes three kinds of samples: convenience, judgment and quota. This method is less time-consuming and less expensive to perform. To operate a convenience sample, you or whomever you hire must assemble the respondent pool, which will recruit the most available population members. A judgment sample simply uses the best judgment of the person selecting those in the pool. These participants will provide the best information. Quota samples require you or the researcher you hire, find and interview a predetermined number of individuals in a number of categories, such as empty-nesters, middle income young singles, or small town executives.

Step 3: Select the response situation.

The most common response situations take place face to face through personal interviewing or by mail, telephone, email, or Internet. Face-to-face and individual interviews, as well as focus groups, are the methods that provide the most flexibility. You can add additional questions as you identify areas that require greater clarification. For example, you may gather information by observing body language. If you conduct the interview yourself, this can be cost-effective, but if you need to hire researchers and professional interviewers, this can become expensive. You also need to be careful when you use interviewers as they bring with them the human factors of bias and distortion.

Telephone interviews work best for gathering information quickly. These interviews contain some of the advantages of a face-to-face interview, such as the ability of the interviewer to add more probing questions, and have a greater respondent rate than direct mail. The disadvantages include the need for brevity. Direct mail questionnaires are the best way to reach individuals in your target pool who did not want to participate in an individual interview or focus group interview. Email has many of the same features as mail, but it may provide faster responses. On the downside, email questions must be completely clear and straightforward, not open to interpretation. Also, the response rates can be low and may be extremely slow. LinkedIn on the Internet provides you with the ability to target your pool, ask questions and get responses. However, it also is important, in this medium, that the questions are clear and understandable. Keep the questions short and to the point. LinkedIn functions proved helpful during my exploration around the topic of health care reform.

Be aware that consumers may not know what they want until they see, or experience it. Sometimes the best focus study subjects are your employees. It was Sony's engineers who first suggested marketing the Sony Walkman to the consumer. Not only was the sound quality superior to anything on the market, it would appeal to consumers who wanted to listen to their music on the go.

When Sony introduced the Sony Walkman in 1979, personal tape recorders had been around for a long time. It was not a new concept, and not a new product. What it was however, was a new experience, mostly due to the quality of the sound and the portability of the device. Unlike other tape recorders the Walkman did not record sound and it had no speakers, only two jacks for earphones – one for the owner and another for a friend to listen if they cared to. The "record" button said "mute" so the listeners could stop the song and talk if they wanted to.

The Sony Walkman was all about "my music," and privacy. It wasn't the product that made the difference. It was the marketing. The Walkman wasn't marketed to journalists or business professionals who used recorders for work. It was marketed to consumers who loved their music and wanted to take it with them. It didn't have recording or speaker capability, but it did have an incredibly good sound, and it was lightweight and totally portable. People could walk around with this device, listening to their music without affecting anyone else. Reviewers laughed at them, saying it would never sell. But within one month of launching 30,000 units of the product it was sold out. Production could not keep up with demand.

In fact, over ten years the Walkman not only became part of our language; the device sold 50 million units, more than any other tape recorder of its time. Today no one thinks anything of the iPod, or iTouch or MP3 players who do the same. It took Sony engineers paying attention to market trends to see an opportunity and push it. They attribute market insights rather than technology for their decision to manufacture the Walkman.

Step 4: Prepare the interviews

The most important thought to keep in mind as you develop the questions is that each must answer, "What do I want to know?" and "What is the objective of my research?" This five-step process will help to develop your questionnaire or discussion guide:

Step 1: Understand what to measure (profit, customer satisfaction, growing customer base, customer, stakeholder and employee satisfaction, units sold, demand etc.)

Step 2: Develop questions to draw out the needed information

Step 3: Make questionnaire decisions about the order, wording and layout

Step 4: Use a small sample to ensure question clarity and to make sure that you have not missed anything (e.g., use this as a test on friends who are not involved with this project.)

Step 5: Make any necessary changes to the test. If the changes prove significant, conduct a questionnaire or discussion guide retest.

Keep in mind that developing these tools is more art than science. Later in this chapter, a more in-depth look at running focus groups will be provided. Taking the time to ensure you have created a well-developed question will save you both time and money in your data collection efforts.

Step 5: Conduct the interviews or groups.

This can be a time-consuming and expensive effort. Make sure to work efficiently and accurately. If errors are going to occur, this is the phase where they will appear.

Step 6: Analyze the results.

Once the data is in hand, the real work begins as you start to analyze and turn this data into usable information. If this is qualitative data, begin to develop your mythology to tabulate the data. If the data is quantitative, statistical techniques and decision models work best to pull essential information from the data.

Referring to our earlier example of the food tours, here is an example of the concept statement and specific questions that might accompany it.

Photographs in the storyboards are licensed from istockphoto.com

Of course, there are pros and cons to this type of research as well.

Pros

- Fast, easy and relatively inexpensive

- Screens out bad ideas

- Uses proven market research technology

- Small samples protect confidentiality

- Provides an array of information

Cons

- Respondents may not understand more abstract concepts

- Requires skillful interviewing

- No statistical validity will exist if the sample is small

- May prove risky since a bad idea may get an okay to proceed

Once the data is analyzed and transformed into solid information, it is time to conduct a review to see if modifications to the concept statement need to be made. If you do make changes, return to the screening process. Take the newly modified concept back through all the screens to make sure the changes meet all the screening criteria. Once rescreened, the concept can be rerun through the research process.

You will quickly learn from concept testing that very rarely will there be a clear "go" signal from this stage, however, you will note some clear "no go" signals.

To move forward most effectively and develop your research, the section below details some of the elements necessary to collect in order to develop your questions, as well as the procedure necessary to execute a successful group. The discussion guide, briefly mentioned earlier in this chapter, is a good place to start. This guide will help you develop an effective tool appropriate for your specific project.

Discussion Guide

To build this discussion guide, follow these seven steps:

Step 1: Determine the objective.

For a discussion guide to be effective, it is very important clearly communicate what you want the group or individual interviews to accomplish. This will guide the development of your questions. Answering the following questions may help with this step: 1) How will you use the information? 2) Who will use the information? 3) On which areas of this concept do you want the most feedback? 4) What specific information do you want to secure from these interviews?

Step 2: Find out what you already know.

If for a new concept, there may not be much information available to review. For other topics, review primary as well as secondary sources about the topic. For instance, if you want to know what travelers think about culinary travel, conduct an Internet search to discover some of the current product or service and read any articles you can locate about the topic. Use this information to frame your questions so they are more specific, or tap into areas that you had not previously considered. Make sure that you develop a solid foundation for each question.

Note: A solid foundation for the question makes sure the question is open-ended, the question is not leading someone to answer in a certain way, and the question leaves the interviewer with the ability to probe the interviewee for more in-depth responses.

Step 3: Develop your first draft.

With the information you gathered going through the first few steps, apply that knowledge to develop a list of questions that answer the "What do I want to know?" question. Focus only on the most important questions. You will have approximately one and one and one-half hours to work through your questions.

Note: When a professional agency performs the recruiting, they will be specific about the time required and will note the amount of compensation paid to each member of a group. If it is a group that you recruit yourself, demonstrate respect for each person's time and conduct the group as efficiently as possible. Keep in mind that people have their own schedules and have limited attention spans.

The final set of questions should consist of five or six major questions accompanied by a few deeper, more probing questions to go along with each. For your first draft, do not limit the number of questions you include. The goal is to design questions that will pull out the information you want to know. What seems to work well is to develop as many as 24 questions. Gradually eliminate and combine that first group of questions until you whittle it down to roughly twelve key questions. Informally test these twelve questions to determine which seem to work best, then make any necessary modifications. After you conduct this informal test and you make the necessary modifications to the selected twelve questions, you are now ready to create a more formal test. The questions you choose will prove most effective if they are open-ended (not yes or no type questions) and range from general to specific.

Step 4: Receive feedback regarding the twelve questions.

Give your initial draft to your test group; this could be team members or others you trust. Ask for their thoughts about which questions capture the fundamental nature of your interview objectives. This step is important to ensure your questions make sense and are appropriate for what you are trying learn.

Step 5: Refine your discussion guide.

Refine your interview questions using the feedback from your test group, then pare down the list to five or six. Remember to use only open-ended questions that proceed from general to specific. For instance, using the culinary travel example, you may ask first, "What images or ideas does the term 'culinary travel' bring up for you?" Simply asking, "What have you heard, or what do you know about culinary travel?" gives your group the chance to say, "Nothing," or "not much." Force them to dig deeper. Even if they have no idea what culinary travel is, asking them to talk about what they think it means will get good first impressions – the kind of first impressions any consumer who isn't familiar with the term will think as well.

The goal of the first question is to get those being interviewed thinking about the topic – culinary travel. Another goal is to provide some insight into what the interviewees know about this topic, their views about it, and how they arrived at those views. Give people time to get their minds and bodies into the same space. As interviewees will arrive from offices, from their homes or from other locations, they may need assistance to help focus their thoughts. They may require additional information as they respond to the first question. For example, for "What have you heard about culinary travel?" you might add, "From your readings" or "As your friends or those at work may have mentioned." If they haven't heard or read anything, encourage them to imagine what it might be like based on the name.

Step 6: Complete a second-round review of the discussion guide.

After you polish the interview questions, return to your team or trusted others to do a final review to gain additional feedback and modifications.

Step 7: Make your last changes and finalize the interview guide.

This interview guide now becomes a "script" for you or your hired moderator / facilitator to use.

Always incorporate basic information, such as ground rules and objective, at the beginning of your script or discussion guide. The following section will provide details regarding how to set up and how to conduct individual and group sessions.

Individual or Group Interview Setups

Consent Process

Consent forms are required for focus groups and individual interviews. All participants should complete these forms in advance. Below is an example:

Consent to participate in a group discussion as part of XYZ Travel Co. research

The purpose of this group dialogue and the character of the questions have been explained to me.

I consent to take part in this group about my experiences purchasing and participating in vacations and tours. I also consent to be tape-recorded and/or videotaped during this group discussion. My involvement is voluntary and I understand that I am free to leave this group at any time.

None of my experiences or thoughts will be shared with anyone outside XYZ Travel Co.

_____   _____
PLEASE PRINT YOUR NAME   DATE

_____
PLEASE SIGN YOUR NAME

Thank you for agreeing to participate. We are very interested to hear your valuable opinions about the concepts presented to you today.

- The purpose of this study is to learn your opinions about culinary tours.

- The information you provide is completely confidential. Your name will not be associated with anything you say during this interview or focus group.

- We would like to tape this interview or focus group to make sure the thoughts, opinions and ideas we hear are captured. No names will be attached to the interview or focus group members and any recorded tapes will be destroyed as soon as they are transcribed.

  (**Note:** If you hire a professional to conduct the groups, along with securing a group recruiter and an interview facility, you may also have video and a mirrored window available for observation. If that is the case, you must notify the individuals or the group.)

- You may refuse to answer any question or withdraw from the study at any time.

- We trust that you understand how important it is that this information is kept private and confidential.

- If at any time you have any questions, now or after you have completed this interview, please feel free to contact ___. (Provide the contact information)

- A short agreement for you to sign must be completed.

  This brief outline, or sample script can be used whenever you host a focus group:

Introduction:

- Welcome

  Introduce yourself, and, if you have a note taker in the room, introduce that person as well. During this introduction, circulate the sign-in sheet, which should contain a few short demographic questions (e.g. age, gender) and a question focused on the concepts, such as, "How many tour type vacations have you experienced?"

- Review:

    ◦ Who "we" or you are and what goal the session should fulfill

    ◦ What will be done with this information

    ◦ Why they were asked to participate

- Explanation of the process

    Ask the group or individual if anyone in the group has ever participated in an interview or focus group before.

- Discuss the function of the interview or focus groups

    ◦ We learn from you (both positive and negative information)

    ◦ We are not trying to achieve consensus, but merely are gathering information

    ◦ There is no virtue in long lists; we are looking for priorities

    ◦ For this concept, we are doing both face-to-face and focus group interviews. The reason for using both of these tools is to get as much in-depth information as possible. These interviews and groups will allow us to understand the context behind the answers provided and help us explore various topics in more detail.

- Basic information

    ◦ The interview/focus group will last about one hour

    ◦ Feel free to move around

    ◦ Provide "housekeeping" details like bathroom and exit locations

    ◦ Help yourself to refreshments (if available)

- ◦ Turn off cell phones if possible

- Ground Rules

    - ◦ Have fun

    - ◦ Everyone should participate

    - ◦ Information provided to those in this focus group must be kept confidential

    - ◦ Focus on the topic, and avoid side conversations

Turn on tape recorder (video device)

- Before the discussion begins, ask the individual or group if there are any questions; if there are, immediately address those questions.

- Introductions – Use an icebreaker, but keep it simple. As an example:

    - ◦ Go around the table and have participants provide their names,

    - ◦ Tell their best ever vacation experiences, as well as their favorite foods, favorite restaurants, etc.

- Begin the discussion

    - ◦ Make sure everyone has a turn

    - ◦ Proceed slowly

    - ◦ Use probing question after asking your initial main question

    - ◦ When you begin to receive repeat answers, move to the next main question or additional probes

- The key roles to be played during the interview session are the facilitator and the note taker

- Facilitators must:

    ° Have excellent listening skills

    ° Have excellent observation skills

    ° Create dialogue among diverse groups and individuals

    ° Remain impartial (i.e., this is particularly important if you conduct the interview yourself) and not give personal opinions about topics (This can influence what people say. You want to know what they think as you already know what you think.)

    ° Engage everyone to be involved

    ° Keep any individual from dominating the conversation

    ° Be sensitive to potential issues

- Responsibilities of the facilitator:

    ° Keep participants focused, engaged, attentive and interested

    ° Manage time effectively

    ° Use prompts and probes to stimulate discussion

    ° Use the discussion guide effectively to ensure all topics are covered

    ° Enforce ground rules

    ° Make sure everyone participates

- Limit side conversations

- Encourage one person to speak at a time

- Explain or restate questions as needed

After the interview or group

Work with the note taker to debrief on the discussion immediately after each focus group. This will ensure the capturing of data and information.

- Note takers must have:

  - Excellent listening skills

  - Exceptional observation skills

  - Superior writing skills including hand writing, grammar, and spelling; their notes are complete but not word-for-word

  - The ability to follows the discussion guide as a form for the note taking

  - The ability to act solely as an observer, never as a participant

  - Impartiality; as a note taker, they must do no creative editing, just record what is said. Again, they are never to participate in the discussion

Example:

The culinary travel concept below demonstrates how the entire process flows. For this purpose, the example was abbreviated to provide a feel for the process and the work required to successfully execute your research. For the culinary travel business, three concepts will be tested. For the sake of this example, the focus will be on the concept of "Food Enthusiasts."

1. Develop your concept statement. This task was completed as shown:

STORYBOARD | **The Food Enthusiasts**

Travel nationally and internationally with a small group of fellow food enthusiasts to experience regional cuisine. Learn from local chefs and experience hands-on preparation and cooking techniques for local dishes.

Experience local culture and customs.

The Food Enthusiasts' tour handles all transportation and accommodations for a fixed price of between $2k to $9k.

Photographs in the storyboards are licensed from istockphoto.com

2. Conduct online research to gather information and answer some of your questions. This research may also reveal more questions for which you will want answers. A quick Internet search turned up a number of interesting magazine articles, a trade publication which provided demographic details, as well as details about customer needs and wants. In addition, a number of potential competitors and their culinary travel offerings surfaced. Remember to review your concept development sheets to see which competitors you identified in your initial research.

3. Define the respondent group(s). My favorite tool is geode-mographics. To learn about this topic, two books provide an outstanding introduction: *The Clustering of America*[7] and ***The Clustered World***,[8] both by Michael Weiss. The Nielsen PRIZM®10 offers a set of geodemographic segments within the United States. This was developed by **Nielsen** and can be found at www. MyBestSegments.com.www[9]

You can take the Nielsen PRIZM® for a "test drive" or become a subscriber. If your product is not intended for consumers, but for industry, you must identify potential product users and their profiles according to possible job category, firm size, region of the country and various other parameters.

Regarding the PRIZM® segmentation profiles in our example, by using this tool, the "Food Enthusiasts" team found a few clusters or segments of individuals to recruit appropriate for interviews and group discussion. If you employ a professional recruiter, turn these profiles over to the recruiter, who then would be respon-sible for filling the interview schedule. These are the segments:

#	SEGMENT NAME	US HOUSEHOLDS	% OF US HOUSEHOLDS	MEDIAN HOUSEHOLD INCOME	AGE RANGE
03	Movers and Shakers	1,845,997	1.55%	$100,739	45-64
05	Country Squires	2,196,181	1.84%	$102,928	35-54
11	God's Country	1,767,383	1.48%	$83923	45-64
14	New Empty Nests	1,197015	1.00%	$69,632	65+

---

7 *The Clustering of America, Michael J. Weiss,*Harper & Row, 1988
8 *The Clustered World, Michael J. Weiss Little Brown and Company* 2000
9 Note: I would especially like to thank the Office of the General Council the Nielsen Company, and Associate General Counsel Robin Kaver in particular for their assistance in providing the data for this section.

This graph shows only some of the readily available website information. For example, who are these potential consumers? What do they
enjoy? Where do they shop? What do they read?

4. Pick the pool. Since the team operates on a limited budget, the
   team members themselves will recruit individuals for the interviews and the group discussions. However, the group decides to
   spend some funds on PRIZM® and develop screening questions
   based on PRIZM® segmentation information. They will use these
   questions as they query each individual. If, after questioning, a
   candidate fits the profile, he will be selected as an interviewee
   until fifteen and twenty individuals.

5. Select the kind of interviews, which can be group, or one-on-one
   interview. The team chooses to conduct two group discussions
   each consist of eight people. The remaining interviews will be
   face-to-face.

6. Prepare for the interviews (and the discussion guide)

   a. How will you use the information obtained?

   To develop our prototype or test market.

   b. Who will use the information?

   Our team will use the data collected.

   (**Note:** In large corporations, the data collected may be used
   by the project sponsor, key executives, and our team and
   by outside consultants.)

   c. Which areas of the concept warrant the most research
   time? The answer depends on:

   ◆ What are the best tour sites?

- What are the tour components?

- What makes up an ideal group?

- How much time is allocated?

- Is this a premium or a discounted tour?

- What information do you want to gain from the research?

- What tour site would create the most demand from potential customers?

- What are all the components of this tour? Some are apparent, but which are not so obvious? What do customers consider important?

- What would make our tours better than any other tour offering?

- What makes our culinary tour so unique that customers would want to return?

- To price these tours at a premium cost (as this pricing yields the largest margins), what would customers expect from each tour?

- If we offer the tour at a lower price (which provides lower margins but more volume) what tour highlights would attract customers most?

d. What do we already know?

From our research, we have an idea about our competition, ideal pricing, locations and the elements for these tours.

From secondary research and trade publications, we gained information about consumers, including their needs and wants. We know they usually take more than one culinary tour and are interested in tours of different lengths, from three-day weekends to longer trips. This research also indicates that the culinary tour market is on an uptrend.

From PRIZM®, we identified four potential market segments, amounting to more than 7 million households, or 5.87 percent of all households. If our culinary tours can capture one percent of that market, that would be equivalent to approximately 70,000 households. If each sale produces free cash flow (the amount of cash remaining after you have paid all expenses) of $900, the potential market value is $62 million. If XYZ tours can capture one percent of the potential free cash flow that would amount to $620,100. For a small company, that is quite a significant annual income generated from one product line. Please keep in mind that this is only a sample from the segments. Additional segments may be added as the product goes to market. Their addition will increase the number individual and sales from this potential market. (If we use one percent as a starting point, think about the potential for one product or service.)

From the individual segmentation derived from PRIZM® snapshot data, we learn the following information about each of the potential customer segments chosen:

Movers and Shakers

Wealthy older adults without children

The mover and shaker category is home to America's up-and-coming business class. The group is comprised of highly educated, wealthy, suburban, dual-income couples that typically range between the ages of 45 and 64. Given its high percentage of executives and white-collar professionals, a decided business bent exists for this segment. Members of this group rank near the top of those who own a small business and have a home office.

Lifestyle Traits:

- Shop at Nordstrom

- Watch NHL games

- Read Yoga Journal

- Play tennis

- Own a Land Rover or a Range Rover vehicle

Country Squires

Upscale middle-age with children

These wealthiest residents live in exurban America, an oasis for affluent Baby Boomers who have fled the city for the charms of small-town living. In these bucolic communities, noted for their recently built homes on sprawling properties, the families of executives live in six-figure comfort. Country squires enjoy country club sports like golf, tennis and swimming, as well as skiing, boating and biking.

Lifestyle Traits:

- Order from www.Amazon.com

- Vacation at ski resorts

- Read *Shape*

- Watch *The Biggest loser*

- Own a Chevy Suburban Flex Fuel

God's Country

> ### Upscale older adults without kids
>
> During the 1970s, as city dwellers and suburbanites began to migrate further into outlying areas, "God's country" emerged as the most affluent of the nation's exurban lifestyles. Today, wealthier communities exist in the hinterlands, but God's country remains a haven for upscale couples that live in spacious homes. Typically college educated Baby Boomers, these Americans work to maintain a balanced lifestyle that exists between high-powered jobs and laid back leisure.
>
> ### Lifestyle Traits:
>
> - Order from orbitz.com
>
> - Go cross country skiing
>
> - Read *Wine Spectator*
>
> - Watch IndyCar Series
>
> - Own an Acura SUV

New Empty Nesters

Upper-middle mature adults without children

Living on their own with their grown children no longer living at home, the new empty nest residence is owned by upper-middle income older Americans who pursue active - and activist - lifestyles. Most residents are over 65 years old, but they show no interest in a retirement setting. This segment ranks at the top for booking all-inclusive travel packages with Europe at the top of their list of favorite destinations.

Lifestyle Traits:

- Shop at T.J. Max

- Vacation for two plus weeks

- Read *Smithsonian*

- Watch golf

- Own a Cadillac sedan

---

7. Develop the first set of draft questions

8. Review what you previously developed to remember which areas of this concept most require feedback. Also review the information you want to gain from these interviews and how much of the interview or discussion time you want to spend on each section. Allocate roughly sixty to ninety minutes for this session. With this information, hold a team or individual mini-brainstorming session to develop as many as fifty potential questions. After a discussion, pare the questions down to twelve. Here are some samples:

   a. What are the best national and international tour sites?

   b. Which cities for tours are in demand nationally and internationally?

   c. What comprises an ideal group?

   d. What is the duration of the tour?

   e. What is the difference between a premium and a discounted tour?

   f. What tour site would generate the most potential customer demand?

   g. What are all the components of the tour? Some may be obvious, but what parts may not be as obvious?

   h. What do customers deem as important components of the tour?

   i. What would make these tours better than others available?

   j. What makes this culinary tour unique enough to generate return customers?

   k. How important is the dining experience?

   l. How important are the supplier partners and partnerships involved?

9. Receive feedback on these twelve questions

10. In this case, XYZ travel is a small start-up firm in its very early stages. The team questions a number of individuals to receive honest feedback about a specific set of questions and hopes they will obtain the information they want to know. After they received this feedback, the team reconvenes to refine the twelve questions.

11. Refine the twelve questions for the discussion guide to reduce them to five major questions. Include one probing question to ask with each of the five. Be cautious at this point, as it will surprise you how much time it will take to discuss only a few questions.

    a. For a culinary tour, what national and international regions interest you?

        ◆ What US cities or regions would you find interesting?

        ◆ What international cities or regions would you find interesting?

        ◆ Is there one place that you must visit on this tour?

    b. What do think about the components of the tour?

       (**Note:** *Use your storyboard when you ask this question.*)

        ◆ What do you think about studying with local chefs?

        ◆ What does the phrase, "hands-on experience," mean to you?

        ◆ Would it appeal to you to prepare local dishes? Why or why not?

        ◆ What does the phrase, "experience local culture," mean to you?

        ◆ What other places or things would you like to see, do or experience during your tour?

    c. How interested are you in other locations and services with which the tour organizer partners?

        ◆ How important are the types of hotels selected and their quality?

- How important are the types of airfare, like whether or not business class or direct flights are available?

- How important is the chef's reputation?

d. If you participated in a culinary tour, who would make your ideal fellow tour companions?

- Would you have a particular demographic preference?

- Would these members share similar interests?

- Would they already possess culinary arts knowledge as beginners or experts?

- What other traits would they have?

e. What would you consider the proper length for a culinary tour?

- How long should a national tour last?

- How long should an international tour last?

- Is a weekend tour long enough or too short?

12. Second-round review. If you work in a larger corporation, once again you will work to engage the project sponsor, managers and executive(s) in the review process. For the team at XYZ travel, the team will question the same reviewers who provided the feedback on the first twelve questions earlier.

Once the feedback is received and any changes incorporated, you can begin to develop your final discussion guide.

13. Make final changes and finalize the discussion guide.

Before you proceed further, review the section on individual or group interview setups. The smooth running of a group will help to set a professional tone, which helps with your data gathering efforts.

Depending on your budget, research and focus group centers are available to do everything for you - for a price. If you do this on your own, begin to recruit the focus group participants. When you start this process, make sure to represent your segment. In fact, you may want to slightly over-recruit to compensate for no-shows, allowing you to retain a critical mass of participants for both the groups and individuals. After everyone arrives, begin the interviews and collect the data. Make sure to reserve physical space for these groups. Recruit the groups that meet you criteria. If possible, provide a room with a one-way mirror, recording devices and technicians to run the equipment. Also arrange to provide food, pay participants and transcribe the data.

If you cannot finance that type of setting, you will need a space at least large enough to accommodate the group, a table – preferably a round one, a tape recorder or a person to take notes and some basic refreshments (beverages and a light snack). The form you developed for effective note taking should also be available. What seems to works best is to list discussion guide questions, listing one per page, along with their probes. Leave enough space between each question to take notes. Several books and online resources can provide additional guidance on running groups if you feel you need additional insights and helpful hints.

To run individual interviews, which should be done first, find a reasonably quiet place ideal for two or three people to talk privately. This would include – the interviewee along with the person doing the interview as well as, ideally, another person to record the data. For this to be beneficial, no matter where the interview is held, the data must be recorded.

From these interviews you will obtain the hard data necessary to convert into useful information. This information is critical in order to move some concepts forward. Some information will need to be modified, rescreened and retested, while other information will disappear. After concept modification and rescreening, run another round of concept tests. This process can sometimes go through a number of rounds prior to advancing to the next stage. For the example of the food enthusiast, the team underwent two rounds of testing before it was clear they had adequate information to proceed to the next stage – prototype development.

Things to consider at this point

Some important observations can be made at this stage. If this is a team effort, you will eliminate some team member ideas at this point. Be very careful how you handle the death of an idea. When you kill an idea, make sure you do not lose the team member along with their idea. Make time to hear all the arguments and explain how each idea was reviewed fairly before moving on. After you modify the concept, then rescreen and retest it, if concept reception still falls into a gray area between whether to continue with it or to discard it, you need to decide which is best. This can be a hard call. If you have years of experience behind you, and your gut feeling is to move ahead, it is worth a try. If you or the team lack that experience and are not sure, it may be better to kill these marginal ideas early.

One of several things can happen next. Perhaps no concept makes it through the concept test, so you or your team needs to return to the idea stage to develop an additional three concepts and start the process anew. Another possibility is you may have a good concept, but find it difficult, for any number of reasons, to test as a prototype.

If this concept is deemed solid by both you and your team, and the risks associated with taking it to market are minimal, you may want to go directly to market. If you work in a regulated industry where you must meet state and federal rules, and must file documents with the state and federal offices before you run a full market test. Once you have filed with the appropriate state or federal agency, your competition will receive notices about what your new product or service will be. Regulated product or service concept testing must be detailed and comprehensive in order for that product/service to go directly to market once filed.

If funding resources exist and you can construct it yourself, your next step is to create a good working prototype. For XYZ travel, a full version of the culinary tour and test the prototype can be developed easily. If your product is more difficult to understand and would be understood better through a functional demonstration model, it is best to build a prototype.

During the research phase, your patience will be tested and, at times, you will feel like you have your lost direction and momentum as ideas that undergo tests fail. However, you will feel enthusiastic when your research uncovers something very valuable and unexpected, or when a concept passes a test. Sometimes you will be pleasantly surprised, while other results will lead to disappointment. No matter what, remain focused on your goal.

If you are creating your project as you read this, now is the time for you to develop your own research. Follow the steps outlined in this chapter to get started. Begin by answering the questions found at the beginning of the chapter:

- Who is your market?

- What are some of the elements required for this type of market research?

- How attractive is the market?

- What opportunities exist?

- How attractive is each opportunity?

- Which research methods are best?

- How do you prepare to do the research?

- How do you test the concepts?

- What am I trying to learn from this concept testing?

- How do you develop a discussion guide for your project?

- How do you run a group session for your project?

- How do you collect data for your project?

- What you do with the data for your project?

C H A P T E R   8

To market, to market

"You've got the eggs in you; the world is fully ready
to celebrate the chicks out of your laying labor.
Never give up. Go and breed. Breed great dreams."
~ISRAELMORE AYIVOR, GHANA AUTHOR

Your product or service now has made it through the concept test stage. By this point, rough estimates of the product's financial potential should start to shine through. The more expensive the product is to develop from this point on, the greater the risk. The greater the risk, the more time and effort required to develop the product's financial viability. If this is a physical product and you work for a large company, the research and development or engineering group will review the concept idea and turn it into one or more prototypes. If you work on your own and have funding, you may choose to use an independent design or engineering firm for assistance to develop your prototype. The last option is to do it yourself.

Before you consider bringing your prototype to market, consider some questions. Like the questions in previous chapters, consider them as you read, then answer them after you finish this chapter:

Innovation process flow

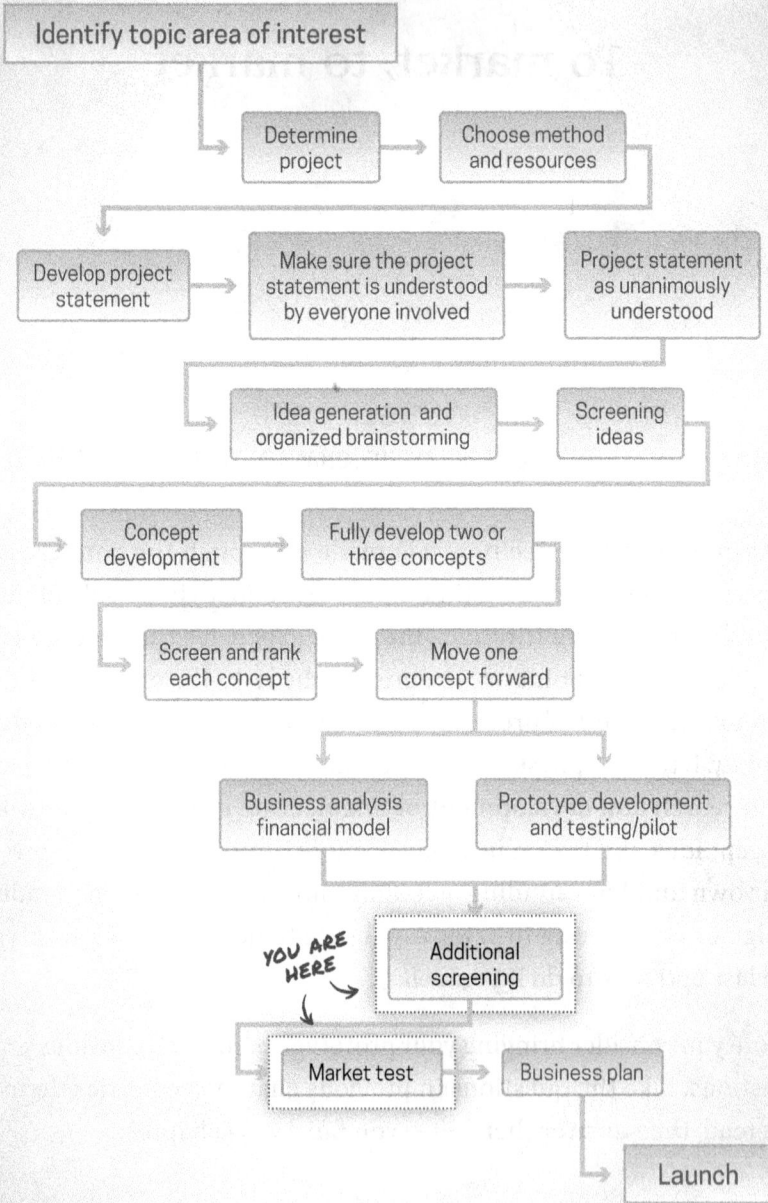

Identify topic area of interest

Determine project → Choose method and resources

Develop project statement → Make sure the project statement is understood by everyone involved → Project statement as unanimously understood

Idea generation and organized brainstorming → Screening ideas

Concept development → Fully develop two or three concepts

Screen and rank each concept → Move one concept forward

Business analysis financial model

Prototype development and testing/pilot

YOU ARE HERE → Additional screening

Market test → Business plan

Launch

- Why should you test your prototype?

- How much time will it take to develop the prototype?

- How much will it cost to develop prototypes?

- Is it necessary to screen the prototype or is it okay not to screen?

- Is a rough financial model necessary?

- What are the product testing alternatives?

- What steps are involved in prototype testing?

- What are the pros and cons when it comes to testing the prototype?

To establish a visual understanding of where we are in the process of creating the million-dollar business idea, see the diagram below to help identify your current position in the progress. The gray boxes will be the focus of this chapter and the next.

Prototype development

Prototype development entails the construction of a working model of the final product or service. At this point, you need to be certain the product or service idea actually can be created physically, efficiently manufactured or developed, and, if a physical product, it performs safely. Also investigate to ensure it provides the stated value proposition contained in the concept statement when before it is delivered to a customer.

Depending on the kind of product, its physical size, and the newness of the technology, prototyping, can take a tremendous amount of time and be very expensive. Boeing's new 787 Dreamliners took years to develop. Complicated analytical software tools can take a year or more, while other ideas may just take months or weeks. On the uncomplicated and inexpensive end of the product development spectrum, such as a child's game may take only a day or several hours to create.

Actually, building prototypes is often more difficult than dreaming up the ideas. When taking concepts from a description, sketch, or a clay model and turning them into a working model, the R&D people, the engineers, and the model builders can face many challenges. If you ever have created even a small project, taking it from the thinking stage, to paper, through execution, it rarely works exactly as planned. The prototype, once in development, must be designed to meet certain functional requirements, as well as meet the needs and perceptions of the target audience, such as size, weight, color, taste, performance, power, etc.

Working models must be tested for functionality. Laboratory and field tests are extremely important, and, depending on the type of product, these can once again range in time length from very long to a relatively short duration. Longer durations, for example, would apply to pharmaceuticals while, on the short end, an example would be the beanbag game.

Tensions may being to wear on the team while you create the prototype, and may extend to the entire firm if you work for a company. Be aware that marketing, research and development, operations, manufacturing, engineering, and other parts of the process will, at times, be at odds with one another.

Just be ready for it to happen and defuse it as much as possible. If you work alone, you will experience an inner tension as the pressure mounts and you near the final test and eventual launch of your product. You will try to balance all the priorities, stay true to the project statement, and still advance the project while trying to maintain some semblance of order in your life.

The information you gather both in the concept stage and the prototype stage is the base data to use in your marketing or business plan. Make sure to keep all of the information organized in a format that can quickly be moved into the next phase of your planning documents.

Remember, the screening process does not stop until you have gone through all the phases of product development. This includes the concept test and the pilot stages. Indeed, based on the information you have been gathering, additional screens should be built that set requirements for the concept or prototype to pass. You also need to tighten existing screens even further, as shown below:

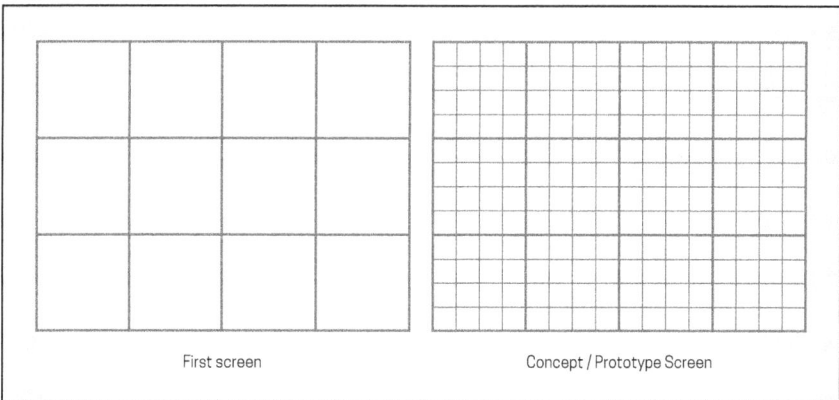

First screen   Concept / Prototype Screen

You now have arrived at the third major stage of the continuous screening process. The gray triangle - labeled screen look the same on the illustration, however keep in mind at each progressive stage the screens become more stringent.

The continuous screening process

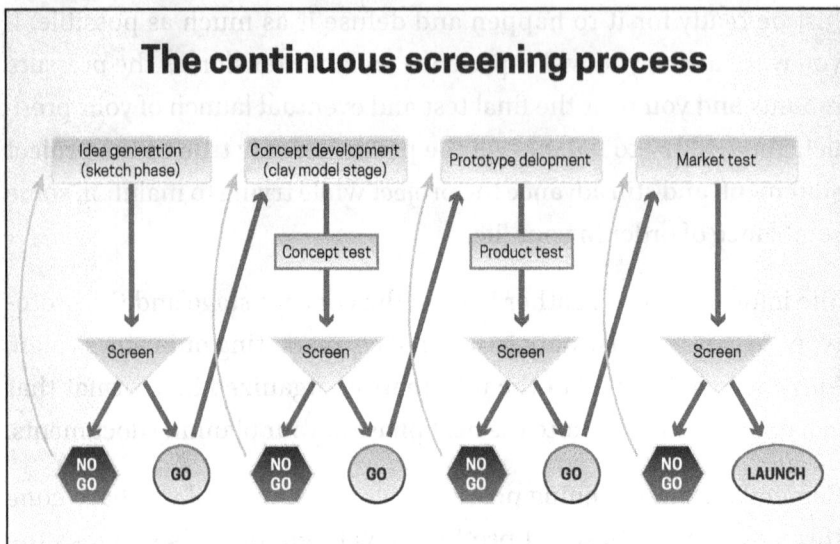

Going back to our culinary travel example and picking up where we left off in the last chapter, by now the team has run two full rounds of concept tests on the culinary travel concept, "The Food Enthusiasts," and recorded the test results in detail. From the information gathered, changes to the concept were made between rounds of testing. In addition, the concept was taken back to the beginning of the screening process and now has passed all screens. The team's work resulted in the final concept that now must be turned into a prototype. Here is the final concept:

The Roman Food Enthusiasts

Travel Internationally to Rome, Italy for seven days and six nights with a intimate group of sixteen fellow food enthusiasts to experience the region's cuisine at some of the best restaurants:

The Pointe Milvio (Trendy), Antica Pesa (Classic), Maccheroni (Trattoria), Roscioli (Enoteca), Motecario (Roman Pizza) and Quinzi & Gabreli (Fish). Learn from visits with noted local chefs. Participate in three-day hands-on experience at the Roman Culinary Institute, cook prepare local dishes and participate in a guided one day market tour.

Experience local history with side trips that include the Colosseum, Pantheon, and St. Peter's Basilica.

The XYZ travel tours handles all transportation, accommodations and gratuities for a fixed price of $6.000.

(Upgrades for business class and first class air fare are available for an additional charge.)

Photographs in these storyboards are licensed from istockphoto.com

The team conducts research in the form of individual interviews, the discussion groups a great deal of information about the prototype will be gained. The prototype description remains necessarily factual since this is not advertising. The point here is to complete your million dollar business idea in order to develop your marketing plan and, if this is your first product, business plan.

In addition, the team has performed some development surrounding expected revenues and expense projections from one trip of sixteen people. Remember, this is only a rough estimate and does not account for any other expenses outside those directly associated with executing the trip. Not included are additional projects overhead, advertising or other expenses assigned to the project. Likewise, no negotiations with suppliers for discounted services have taken place. The goal now is to explore if "The Roman Food Enthusiast Tour" project is worth pursuing.

The following is an example of a simple spreadsheet that shows the value the prototype provides each component:

INPUTS		
Members on the tour	$	16.00
Per person fee	$	6,000.00
Per person airfare	$	2,000.00
Motor coach fee per person	$	70.00
Length of the tour	$	7.00
Hotel nights	$	6.00
Hotel cost per night	$	180.00
Dinners	$	100.00
Lunches	$	25.00
Breakfasts	$	10.00
Tuition	$	500.00
Direct Labor	$	3,000.00

REVENUE		
Per person tour fees total	$	96,000.00
Total Income	$	*96,000.00*
COST		
TRANSPORTATION		
Airfare	$	32,000.00
Motor Coach	$	7,840.00
ACCOMMODATIONS		
Hotel	$	17,280.00
MEALS		
Breakfast	$	672.00
Lunch	$	2,800.00
Dinner	$	9,600.00
INSTRUCTIONAL		
Tuition	$	8,000.00
Direct labor	$	3,000.00
Total Cost	$	*81,192.00*
CASH FROM PROJECT		
Total Revenue	$	96,000.00
- Total Cost	$	81,192.00
Total Cost	**$**	**14,808.00**

These rough financials for the Roman Food Enthusiast suggest the project should continue. In fact, if you execute twelve trips a year, this business would produce gross revenues of more than $1.1 million. As the business moves forward, these financials must be fine-tuned, but, for now, you have established a strong base from which to work.

Product testing option

Quantitative

In-home/in-office usage tests

Depth interviews

Central location intercepts

Focus groups

Qualitative

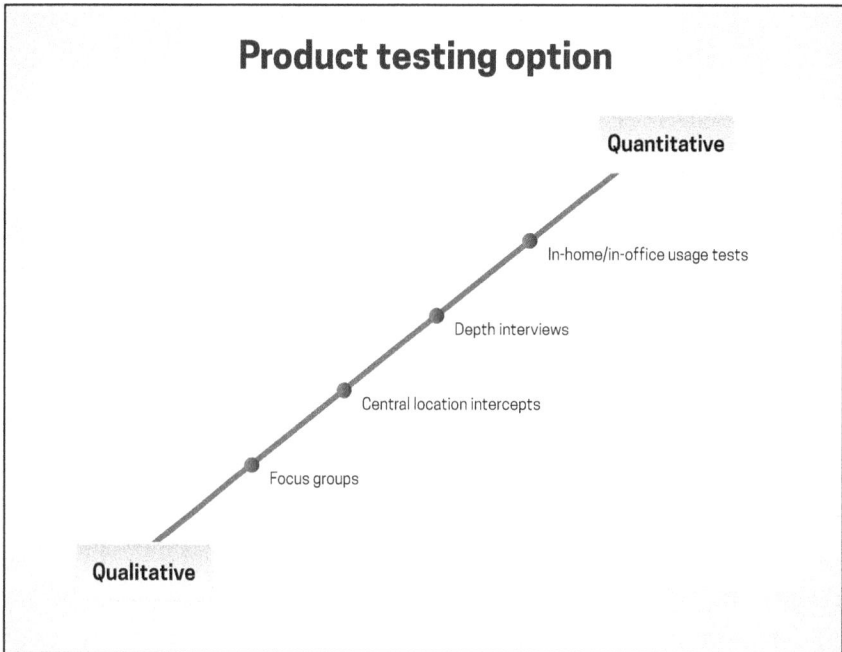

Although similar to what we discussed in chapter seven, product-testing alternatives differ in a few specific ways. When conducted in the office, you may ask the same questions. The testing alternatives in the diagram above illustrate a range of options available to you. Discussion and focus groups, mall and central location intercepts, in-depth interviews, in-home and in-office tests all are part of this research. As with the concept test, you need to determine which testing situation and which research tools best suit your product or service. For culinary travel, most testing models would work well, while testing a large piece of equipment may dictate different testing options. Especially if you have only a small budget, be aware of your options in order to choose wisely the option that is not only affordable, but provides the essential information you need.

For the entrepreneur working on his first idea with little or no budget, it is important to use these same research situations, but also to use friends and hold focus lunches and tests in a private residence. The challenge is to allow the customer to do the talking while you show no bias. Take notes, record the sessions and attempt to capture only the facts; make every effort not to allow your mind to edit the proceedings. It is also important to remember not to reveal your idea. Make choices when you consider (or choose) who to interview and make sure all interviewed agree to keep any information or concepts you provide confidential.

As you enter this phase, keep in mind that what happens here is more art than science. You need to observe carefully any vocal nuances and judiciously observe all respondent the body language. Probe more deeply into what each respondent tells you in order to gain a better understanding and avoid potential traps. For example, you want consumers to purchase your product at least once a week, you may ask, "How many times will you use this product?" If the response is, "On special occasions," you may want to probe further and ask what "special occasions" means to them. If the answer is "only on New Year's Eve and one other day," you may not develop the sales volume for a sustainable product. If the response is "two or three times a week," that is a very positive sign that your product is on the right course.

Your working model will need to function properly. If it does not, and you must continually explain how it works, rather than waste valuable time, time will be better spent if you secure important prototype impressions from your respondents. However, be certain your prototype design supports product performance and delivers on its value proposition.

As you prepare for testing, be sure to follow these six steps, described below:

Steps in product testing

Tabulate
and analyze
results

Conduct
interviews
group and
individual

Prepare
interviews

Select
respondent
situation

Define
respondent
group

Prepare
product
prototypes

Choose
presentation
style:
• Narrative
• Drawings
• Prototype
  (more then
  one)
Decide what
you will
communicate

Early adaptors?
Users?
Demographics?

Face-to-face
Mail
Internet

One-on-one
Group

Choose
content
Avoid bias

Moderate
clearly without
bias

Use a third
party, if
possible

Analysis is best
done within a
group

Proceed
back to
brainstorming
development
stage
  or
Cease
exploration and
development

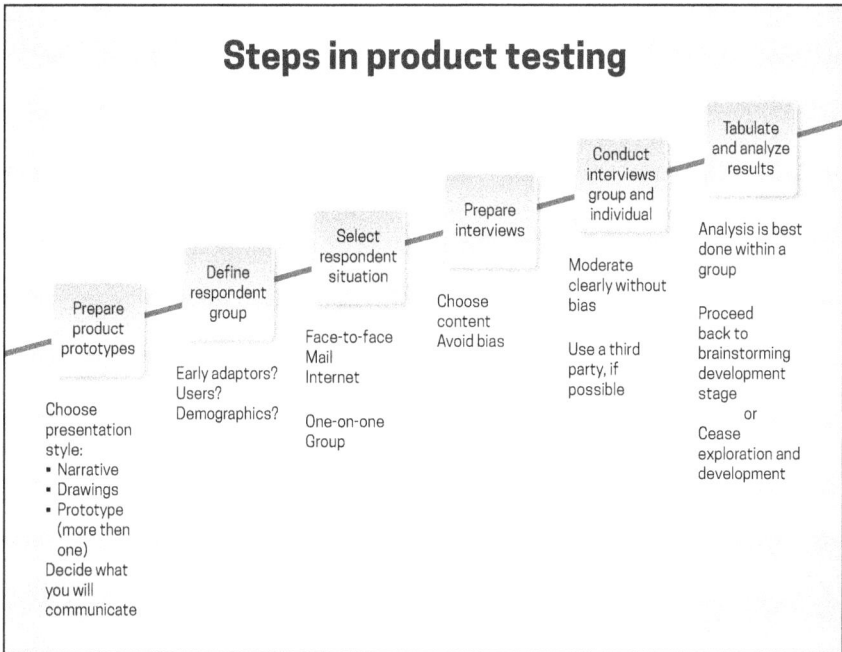

Step 1: Decide which presentation method to use. These include writing a narrative, displaying drawings or creating a working prototype. The selection depends on cost, time and type of product or service.

Step 2: Decide exactly what you want to communicate. Remember, stay fact-focused and avoid creating a sales pitch.

Step 3: Define and choose group members to participate, as well as the type of response situation you will use, as you conduct this prototype testing process. As in an earlier example, we used PRIZM segments for recruiting our groups and individual interviews. At this point, it would further your research not only to use the clusters and individuals from each possible early adopter segment, but also to use those who currently use similar products and services. The more insights you can gain from potential product or service users, the more likely you are to gain important information. If your team is sponsored internally, test the product or service with them as well. Keep in mind that these individuals will be the same ones who will approve or disapprove the funding necessary to forward this project.

Choose your response situation. Determine if you prefer face-to-face conversations, mall intercept encounters, or a discussion or focus group scenario in a home or office setting? At the same time, develop any data collection tools necessary. These include questionnaires the discussion guide, etc.

Recruit targeted respondents as you did for the concept test. Make sure to have a sufficient number of respondents to provide a reliable sample size from which to draw information. When you conduct these interviews, remember to collect the data using whatever method works best for your testing situation. This could include audio or video recording or merely good, old-fashioned note taking.

Step 4: If you are going to use more than one prototype, make sure that your group or individual presentation or demonstration displays no bias. Any bias will taint your research results. Keep in mind you are presenting the facts, Stay away from making a sales pitch.

Step 5: Conduct your interviews and discussion or focus groups. For those doing this research alone, focus lunches and small group discussions may work best. Always ask each respondent group the same questions the same way to ensure all responses pertain to those same questions and probes.

Step 6: Analyze the data gathered. For a number of reasons, this is a team effort. You must make sure everyone hears and understand all the answers. If changes are required, those responsible for these changes should be available to provide feedback or to ask additional clarifying questions. To determine what respondents are really saying, listening skills are critical during this stage. Does the data you collected demonstrate that this product or service delivers on its value proposition? Is the product sufficiently differentiated enough from the competition, both in form and substance, to gain a market advantage? Does this offering meet customer needs and wants?

Once you analyze the test results, how would you rate the response? Did the prototype succeed as a clear winner? Does the prototype need modification? Did it lose? Where the results inconclusive? If it clearly won, it is ready for market. If it clearly lost or, its success is questionable, which frequently happens, examine what you steps you can take to move the project closer to becoming a clear winner. If you make changes, will the changes you make be significant enough to put the prototype through a retest and rescreen?

Product Testing Pros and Cons

Again, both pros and cons to testing your prototype exist. Understanding both will help improve your own testing.

Pros

- Assure product will deliver on the inherent promise in customers

- Assures product can be physically produced

Cons

- The working model prototype may not be as elegant as the final product and may result in the not being fair

- Prototype testing requires skillful interviewing

- If the sample size is too small, the sample may not be the statistically valid

Returning to our culinary travel example, evaluate the Roman Food Enthusiast through the prototype testing stages.

Step 1: Decide which presentation method will work best for the Roman Food Enthusiast. You may remember the narrative and drawing:

The Roman Food Enthusiasts

Travel Internationally to Rome, Italy for seven days and six nights with a intimate group of sixteen fellow food enthusiasts to experience the region's cuisine at some of the best restaurants:

The Pointe Milvio (Trendy), Antica Pesa (Classic), Maccheroni (Trattoria), Roscioli (Enoteca), Motecario (Roman Pizza) and Quinzi & Gabreli (Fish). Learn from visits with noted local chefs. Participate in three-day hands-on experience at the Roman Culinary Institute, cook prepare local dishes and participate in a guided one day market tour.

Experience local history with side trips that include the Colosseum, Pantheon, and St. Peter's Basilica.

The XYZ travel tours handles all transportation, accommodations and gratuities for a fixed price of $6.000.

(Upgrades for business class and first class air fare are available for an additional charge.)

Photographs in the storyboards are licensed from istockphoto.com

Step 2: Decide exactly what information you want to communicate. In the narrative for the Roman Food Enthusiasts, the group made the decision to detail many of the tour components to be sampled, such as its length, the restaurants, the participating chefs, the schools visited, the type and length of each lesson, any side trip locations and the package price.

What about the discussion guide development process? This guide will develop using the same process used to develop the concept statement. The key difference is that the question can be more detail-focused on specific components, while, at the same time, questions may become more global to assess respondent feelings. For example, for questions about the Roman Food Enthusiast prototype, begin globally and develop each question to fill in details.

- What do you like about the Roman Food Enthusiasts' tour?

- What do you see as the positives of this prototype?

- What, to you, is the most important component of this prototype?

- Rank the positives from 1 to 10, with 10 being the top-ranked positive aspect.

- What could improve this concept?

- What are the negatives? Rank these from 1 to 10, with 10 being the top-ranked negative.

- What would you do to change each negative into a positive?

You also may add additional questions like;

- How do you feel about the length of the described Roman Food Enthusiasts Tour? (For each of these questions, circle the option which most describes your feelings.)

1	2	3	4	5	6	7
Dislike Intensely	Dislike	Dislike Slightly	Indifferent	Like Slightly	Like	Like Intensely

- How do you feel about the restaurant choices?

1	2	3	4	5	6	7
Dislike Intensely	Dislike	Dislike Slightly	Indifferent	Like Slightly	Like	Like Intensely

- What are your feelings about the types of food choices?

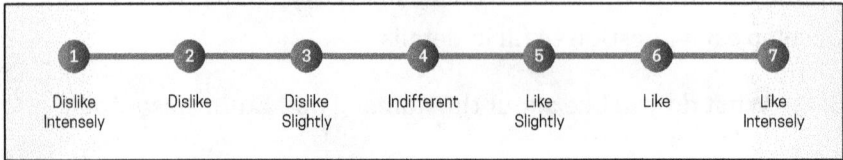

1	2	3	4	5	6	7
Dislike Intensely	Dislike	Dislike Slightly	Indifferent	Like Slightly	Like	Like Intensely

Continue the process, adding new questions developed for each of the components.

Next, ask participants how likely they are to buy your product:

> How interested would you be in purchasing the Roman Food Enthusiasts Tour package if it were available to you at the price of $6,000?
>
> ❑ I would definitely buy
>
> ❑ I would probably buy
>
> ❑ I might or might not buy
>
> ❑ I would probably not buy
>
> ❑ I would definitely not buy

Remember, look for 67 percent of respondents to check one of the first two boxes, "I would definitely buy" and "I would probably buy." This helps to ensure this concept is strong enough to allow you to successfully proceed.

Step 3: Define and choose the group you want to participate in the prototype testing process. Returning to use my favorite tool, the Nielsen PRIZM for geodemographics, one group determined that a few clusters for the "Food Enthusiasts" questions contained individuals who should be recruited for interviews and group discussions. During this round of questioning, the recruiter will ask additional screening questions to qualify each individual. As example of these questions:

- "Have you been to Europe on a tour?"

- "Have you been on a specialty tour in Europe?"

- "Have you ever been on a culinary tour of any kind?"

These questions will help generate participants who have participated in small group tours and, possibly, have experienced culinary tours. Here are the segments we used before:

#	SEGMENT NAME	US HOUSEHOLDS	% OF US HOUSEHOLDS	INCOME	AGE RANGE
03	Movers and shakers	1,864,599	1.61%	$109,351	35-54
05	Country squires	2,005,091	1.73%	$107,442	35-54
11	God's country	1,689,583	1.43%	$88,614	35-54
14	New empty nesters	1,243,807	1.07%	$75,295	65+

To ensure an adequate sample size, the search can be expanded into some of the adjacent PRIZM segments representing similar numbers of households and incomes, such as:

- 04 Young Digerati, age range 24-44

- 06 Winners Circle age range 35-54

- 07 Money and Brains age range 45-65.

If you do this assessment alone, find individuals who have taken tours. Ask friends and family for contacts. Work to develop a sufficient pool of respondents to participate in your interviews. This will ensure you approach the profile of your target customer as closely as possible.

Step 4: If you are going to use more than one prototype, make sure that your group or individual presentations or demonstrations to the display no bias. Since, in this example, only one prototype is being tested, do not worry about a bias between concepts, however the same rules apply that were used to present concepts. Just be careful not to create bias through your word choices or personal reactions. In this example, the team decided to show only the one prototype. If your group determines that the prototype you present does not pass, you will need to make modifications and another pass before the group decides to scrap this one and select another of the final three concepts to turn into a prototype.

Step 5: Conduct the interviews and discussion or focus groups. Refer back to the section called **Individual or Group Interview Setups** in chapter seven for a quick refresher to confirm all details are in order. At this point, the Roman food enthusiast team will run their own discussion or focus groups and gather the data.

Step 6: Tabulate the results from the discussion or focus groups as well as from your individual interviews. Review all recordings as well as all notes to be certain you capture even the smallest details. This team gathered all its information about the prototype and their analysis results showed that many more positives than negatives. Their data also shows no single correct human answer, but the data indicated a trend despite overwhelmingly different individual answers. The feedback overall was positive. The prototype passed the "Would you buy?" test with more than 72 percent of respondents checking either the "I would definitely buy" or "I would probably buy." Most importantly, the team learned that these respondents believed this prototype delivers on its value proposition of culinary travel to learn about food types and instruction about how to prepare regional cuisine. Given these test results, this project will move ahead.

Congratulations to the XYZ team; their million-dollar business idea now exists!

This project now progresses to the next stage. For an existing business, the goal of this stage is to gain project sponsor and management approval. Along with this approval, allocate a budget to the project and develop a marketing plan. Your team now needs to bring the project to the next level and begin the commercialization process. Most existing businesses use an established business model under which the product or service will operate. In fact, this model may have been included in the screening criteria.

The solo entrepreneur must understand this business model, as well as how to build a business plan and how to seek funding. The focus of the next chapter will include a basic review of how to build your business model. After you understand this business model, you may want to read the book ***How to Grow a Great Business and Power Network***[10] by Melissa Giovagnoli and David R. Stover. This book will help you clearly think through all the steps necessary to establish a solid business plan and business. You may find this an invaluable resource that saves you time and energy as it illustrates how to avoid many possible pitfalls.

The path forward, at times, may seem unclear. If you believe your prototype's probable success is less than 50 percent, it definitely needs to be revised and, perhaps, eliminated. Remember, this process is more art than science. Obtain a consensus from your team, if you are working with one, about their feelings. Most percentages tend to be more qualitative than quantitative, so feelings and impressions have a huge impact on final decisions. However, the final decision falls on the team leader.

---

10 *How to Grow a Great Business and Power Network*, Melissa Giovagnoli and David R. Stover Networlding Publications, 2009

Know you are making significant progress on this journey. The idea now becomes an integral part of you. You will have developed a passion for its success. You and the idea have merged. Now you need to stay the course as you work out all the necessary details to commercialize or establish your business. The key to success is to push toward the finish line as hard as you can. However, be careful not to let your passion overcome you. One entrepreneur was so blinded by his belief that only one way existed - his way, that this stubbornness caused him to miss a multimillion-dollar funding opportunity due to a minor concern. Stay focused on the goal and maintain flexible guidelines. Most importantly, always deliver on the value proposition.

Return to the questions found at the beginning of this chapter and answer them based on your specific project:

- How much time will prototype development take?

- How much will prototype development cost?

- Why should I test my prototype?

- Do I really need to screen?

- Is a rough financial model necessary?

- What alternatives exist for product testing?

- What steps are involved in prototype testing?

- What are the pros and cons for testing the prototype?

CHAPTER 9

The next steps

*"His life was one long extravaganza,
like living inside a Faberge egg."*
~ JOHN LAHR, CRITIC

Now that your million-dollar business idea is established, before you begin to work on the marketing plan or business plan, spend some time on another worthwhile step. That step is to understand what business model best fits your idea or comes out of your idea. Below are some questions to contemplate as you read this chapter.

- Where am I in the process?

- What is my next step?

- What is a basic business model?

- What are my processes?

- What are my main resources?

At this point, you are between market testing and developing your complete business plan, represented by the flow chart below.

Innovation process flow

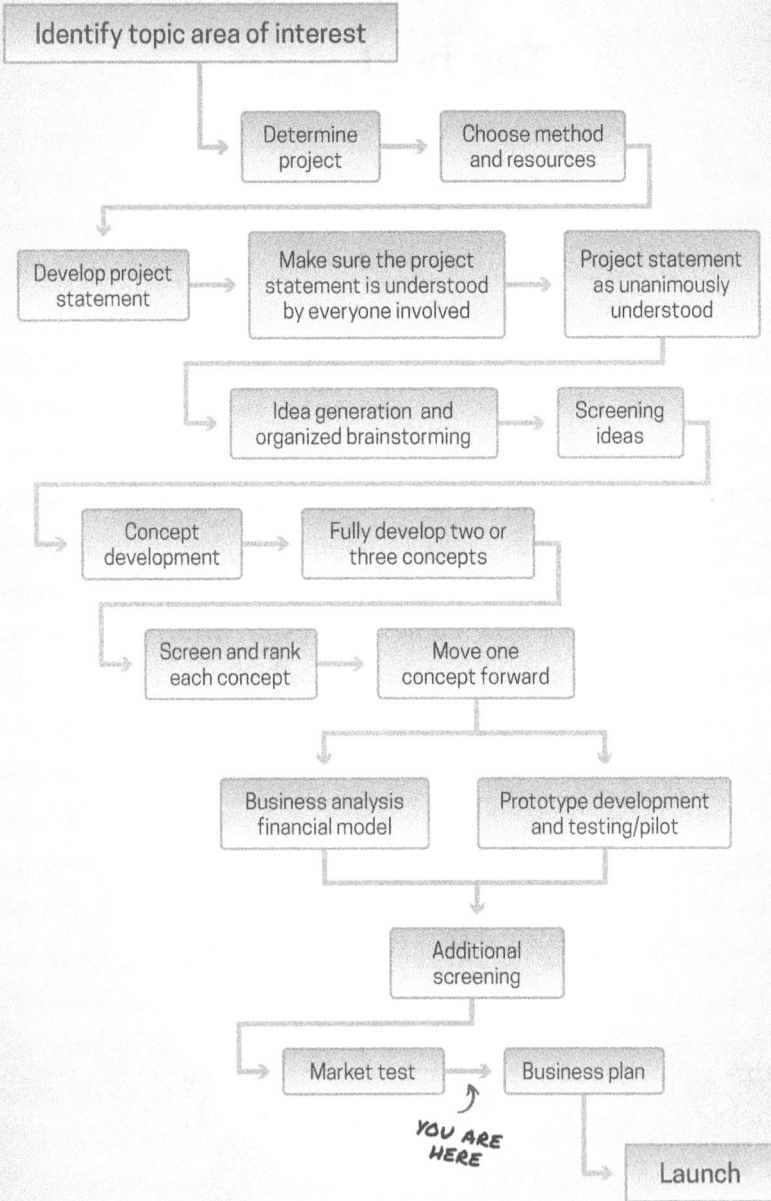

Identify topic area of interest

Determine project

Choose method and resources

Develop project statement

Make sure the project statement is understood by everyone involved

Project statement as unanimously understood

Idea generation and organized brainstorming

Screening ideas

Concept development

Fully develop two or three concepts

Screen and rank each concept

Move one concept forward

Business analysis financial model

Prototype development and testing/pilot

Additional screening

Market test

Business plan

YOU ARE HERE

Launch

Prior to working on your marketing or business plan, when you develop your business model, you will develop some critical insights and some material necessary to facilitate further planning. Business is complicated; even simple businesses are complicated. To help you consider all the issues you may face, it is best to be armed with a method that can assist you with this discussion and consideration.

While the main theme of this book revolves around how to create an idea, over time it became evident that a transition to bridge the idea with the business plan is imperative. This business model development is that necessary step. The goal here is to provide a brief introduction to this topic, along with valuable resources you will find useful as you develop your business model.

These two books can be very helpful during this process:

- *Business Model Generation*[11] by Alexander Osterwalder and Yves Pigneur

- *Seizing the White Space: Business Models Innovation for Growth and Renewal*[12] by Mark W. Johnson.

Also, refer to the companion website to the *Business Model Generation* book, www.businessmodelgeneration.com; if you have an Apple® iPad, there is also a business model App available. These resources offer an excellent source of business model information and provide material that can be downloaded.

To help you better understand your business, a business model contains a number of components, including the value proposition, revenue and costs, processes and your inputs such as knowledge, and skills

11 *Business Model Generation, Alexander Oserwalder & Yves Pigneur,* John Wiley & Sons, 2010
12 *Seizing the White Space: Business Model Innovation for Growth and Renewal,* Harvard Business School Publishing, 2010

resources. Up until now, this book has focused on helping you develop your business idea based on the value proposition, your core idea. If you have followed the process outlined in this book you will already have gathered data to develop your basic business model. Now you will need to pull all the puzzle parts together.

The high level business model puzzle parts are:

Value proposition, or core idea - This refers to the products or services that meet customer needs or wants. Simply put, they solve a customer's problem.

Processes - These would include examples such as manufacturing, sourcing material, problem solving, procurement, supply, maintenance, shipping and storage.

Inputs - These include suppliers, labor, offices, warehousing, computers, computer systems, vehicles, intellectual property, brands, patents, copyrights, equipment, partnerships and alliances as good examples.

Revenue and cost structure - Revenue examples would describe the various types of revenue flows and type low margin or high margin, as well as sources of revenue sales, licensing, and royalties. On the cost side, keeping high level discounts, what rules will be applied and measures will be taken on discounts and volume discounts in your model?

Let's once again look at the "The Roman Food Enthusiasts" tour example, below is a possible business model using our four basic elements.

The value proposition, or core idea, for culinary travel is learning about food types and how to prepare regional cuisines.

Processes - relationships with suppliers, high margin requirements, credit cards, sourcing of high quality travel, hotels, restaurants and culinary schools, direct marketing, Web, mail and advertising, total quality management (TQM), cost control

Inputs - Airlines, bus companies, hotels, chefs, restaurants, culinary schools, data bases, data mining tools, inbound and outbound marketing suppliers, website

Revenue and cost structure - Higher margin personalized service from each event: travel, restaurant or tour, emphasis on high quality, volume discounts from suppliers

If you wanted to go a little deeper into the development of your business model, you may want to add some critical areas to your model. Examples include customer segments, alliance or partnerships and customer relations.

What would your business model look like? What are your high level elements?

Value preposition -

Processes -

Inputs -

Revenue -

Recognizing some of the guideposts along this path should make you more aware of your progress and the reasons you experience various events as they occur. Remember, during your travels you will cycle through your experiences twice. The first will be as you develop your concept – the million-dollar business idea, and the other will be as you go through the business planning, approval and financing process.

You now should be ready to answer the following questions:

- What is my next step?

- Where am I in the process?

- What are some basic business models?

- What is my profit formula?

- What are my key processes?

- What are my main resources?

- What are my major customer segments?

- What are my best channels?

- What actions are integral to my success?

- Who are my main partners?

- What does the road map look like?

This is just the end of the beginning. After all, hatching your idea is the first step.

So many more experiences lie ahead as you grow your beautifully hatched, million dollar business idea into childhood, through its teen years, and then guide it through adulthood. This book is meant to help you hatch that idea, but once the idea has hatched, it is your responsibility to take the next step and develop your business plan. A great resource is the book, *How to Grow a Great Business and Power Network*, so refer to that book as you prepare to take the next step.

Journey on.

APPENDIX A

This appendix contains a set of templates for you to use as you build your million-dollar business idea.

Megatrend template

What megatrends have you discovered during your research?

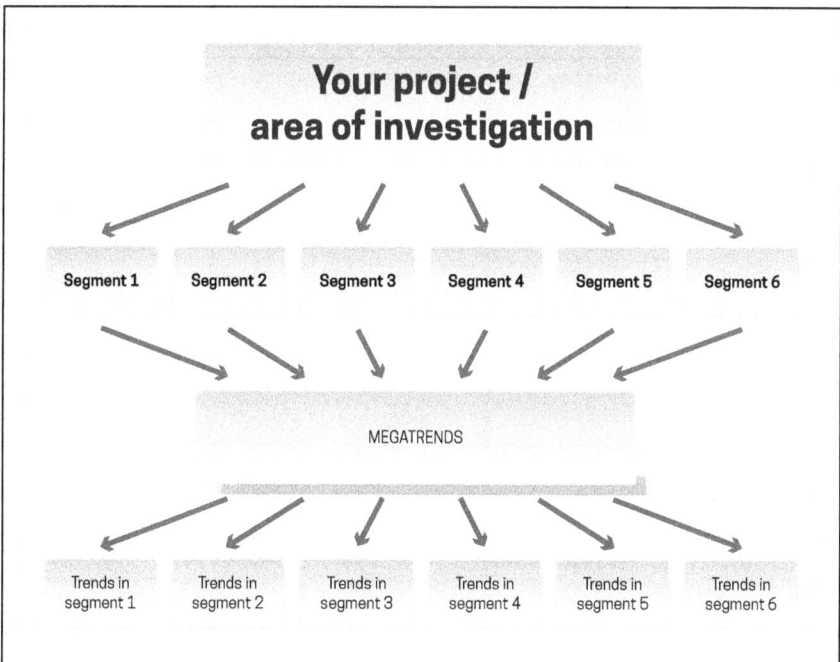

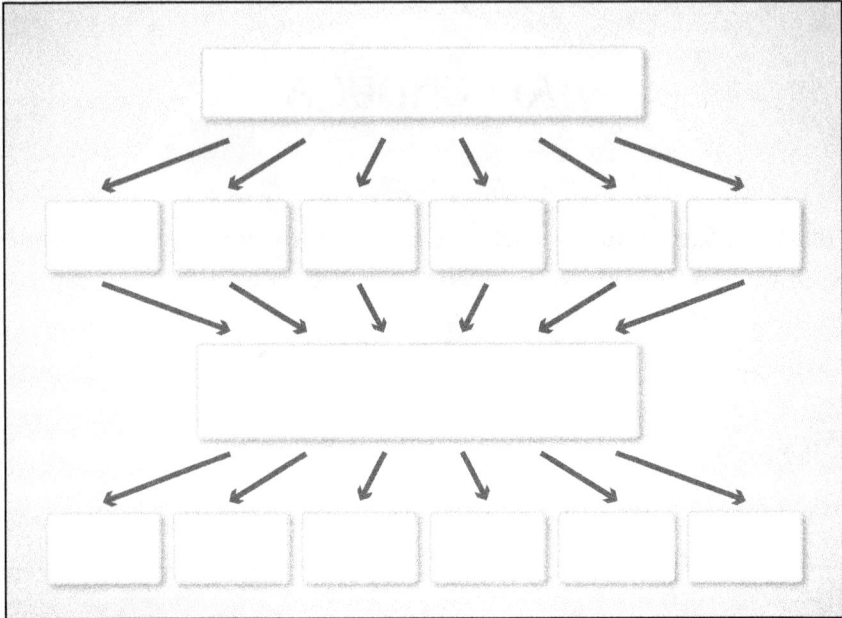

APPENDIX B

Personal fit template

	YES	NO	MAYBE	WHY
Fits my strengths				
Stays away from my weaknesses				
Fits my values				
I have a passion for this area				
This area energizes me				
I can visualize myself doing this				
I will achieve being in the zone, an optimal experience, doing this				
Provides me with the opportunity to approach my ultimate goal				
Allows me the opportunity to approach my sub-goals				
Fits within available resources				
Timeline is realistic				
Other ideas you may want to add				

APPENDIX C

Total concept definition worksheet #1
Core idea definition and development

WHAT IS THE CORE IDEA?	
WHAT DOES IT DO?	
HOW DOES IT WORK?	
WHAT DOES IT LOOK LIKE?	
WHAT ARE THE COMPONENTS?	
WHAT ARE THE BENEFITS?	

Total concept definition worksheet #2
Product / service offering and target prospects

WHAT IS THE CORE OFFERING ? **WHAT IS THE TANGIBLE OFFERING?** **WHAT IS THE AUGMENTED OFFERING?**	Augmented offering Tangible offering Core offering		
WHO ARE THE PROSPECTS?	Target segment 1 ⬇	Target segment 2 ⬇	Target segment 3 ⬇
WHAT ARE THEIR UNIQUE NEEDS?	⬇	⬇	⬇
WHAT DO THE PROSPECTS LOOK LIKE?			

Total concept definition worksheet #3

Who is the competition?

WHAT IS THE VALUE PROPOSITION?		Segment I	Segment II	Segment III
	What are the segment's Value-added offerings?			
	What is the core offering?			
WHO IS THE COMPETITION?	Competitor 1			
	Competitor 2			
	Competitor 3			

Total concept definition worksheet #4

Beginning business case definitions

PRODUCT	
PRICE	
DISTRIBUTION	
PROMOTION	
REGULATIONS	

APPENDIX D

Orange exercise answers

Total concept definition worksheet – The Orange

Core idea definition and development

WHAT IS THE CORE IDEA?	• A sweet tasting food item
WHAT DOES IT DO?	• Tastes good • Nutritious • Colorful and decorative
HOW DOES IT WORK?	• Cut into slices • Squeeze • Peel
WHAT DOES IT LOOK LIKE?	• Round and colored orange • Approximately 4 inches in diameter
WHAT ARE THE COMPONENTS?	• Thick, waxy skin • Vitamin C and niacin • Tasty citrus juice • Pulp
WHAT ARE THE BENEFITS?	• Sweet and tastes good • Thirst quenching • Nutritious vitamin C supplement • Low in calories • Good as a snack

Total concept definition worksheet #2

Product / service offering and target prospects

WHAT IS THE CORE OFFERING ?	Augmented offering · Tangible offering · Fun to eat · Refreshing · Core offering (sweet tasting food) · Satisfies thirst · Versatile Slice Squeezed Peel · Portablet · Nutrition · Pretty color · Requires no information		
WHAT IS THE TANGIBLE OFFERING?			
WHAT IS THE AUGMENTED OFFERING?			
WHO ARE THE PROSPECTS?	Target segment 1 Premium orange buyers	Target Segment 2 Orange eaters	Target Segment 3 Fresh orange juice drinkers
WHAT ARE THEIR UNIQUE NEEDS?	Quality conscious adults	All ages and genders Snack eaters	All ages and genders Health conscious
WHAT DO THE PROSPECTS LOOK LIKE?	• Less seeds • Bright, even color • No bruises • Large size	• Versatile and fun to eat • Easy to pack • Vitamin C supplement	• Refreshing and satisfying • Juicy • Vitamin supplement

Total concept definition worksheet – The Orange
Who is the competition?

WHAT IS THE VALUE PROPOSITION?		Segment I Shipped fruit	Segment II At-home consumer	Segment III Juice producers
	What are the segment's Value-added offerings?	• Large size • Extra fancy • Sweetest taste	• Refreshing • Satisfies thirst • Nutritious	• Ample supply available on demand
	What is the core offering?	• Fresh • Sweet tasting • Uncontaminated • Consistent taste		
WHO IS THE COMPETITION?	Competitor 1 Other citrus fruits			
	Competitor 2 Breakfast cereals			
	Competitor 3 Vegetable snacks			
	(Other competitors: Vitamins, snack food products, decorative accessories and garnishes)			

Total concept definition worksheet – The Orange
Beginning business case definitions

PRODUCT	Sold in single units for snacking or by the pound
PRICE	Per pound; this calculates to approximately $ .89 each, which is comparable to other snack items
DISTRIBUTION	Available at supermarkets, grocery stores, online direct sellers, liquor stores and street corner fruit stands
PROMOTION	Internet sites, television, radio, magazines, direct mail, public relations and discounts for restaurants
REGULATIONS	FDA approval of product, as well as manufacturing and distribution process

Glossary of terms

Affinity Idea Diagram (AID) - Allows organization and capture of the large volumes of ideas from developed brainstorming sessions, helps to capture all the best current thinking , so no ideas are unintentionally lost and allows for more thought patterns to emerge from the proto-idea data through the process of sorting and shaping.

Augmented offer - Detail additional benefits and features that differentiate this product or service from the competition and make it more desirable.

Business model - Is a plan which includes all functions and components of the business as well as revenue flows and expenditures.

Business screen - Uses a combination of elements to screen ideas. Some examples; target market, market size, market potential, product benefits vs. competition, product or service meet previously unmet needs.

Central location or mall intercepts interviews - Individual interviews conducted in high traffic areas.

Channels - The method product or services are delivered. Marketing channels can include wholesalers, transporters, warehouses, dealers, jobbers, retailers, manufacturer representatives, industrial distributers, web aggregators and others.

Cluster analysis - Is used in marketing research by placing individuals or objects into mutually exclusive groups.

Concept statement - Is an expanded version of basic idea explained in meaningful consumer terms. Example the idea is basic transportation; the concept is an environmentally friendly car.

Concept Test - Are used to discover whether or not the concept is worth pursuing or if the concept needs modification before additional testing.

Conjoint analysis - Is used in marketing research to determine the value consumers place on different characteristics of the same product.

Consumer demands - the desire for specific products accompanied by an ability and willingness to purchase them.

Consumer wants - Desires for specific items that satisfy deeper needs. A want is something someone would like to have, even if may not be beneficial.

Core Competencies - are the specific mixture of pooled knowledge and technical capacities that allow a business to be competitive in the marketplace.

Core offering - The basic product or service a firm presents for purchase.

Cost Structure - Inputs are incurred by various elements of a business which than produce outputs. Costs can be view as the sacrifice made for producing products and services.

Customer need - Is something essential to life, such as food, water, shelter, clothing, safety and self-esteem.

Customer Relations - A set of activities provided by the business, which include some of the following examples: self-service, automated service, personal assistance and user communities.

Customer Segments - Customer groupings define by a set of parameters such as demographics, psychographics, media preferences, attitudes, price sensitivity and quality preferences.

Developmental stage - The stage in organized brainstorming process designed to organize, evolve, prioritize large volumes of incomplete ideas, or proto-ideas.

Exogenous variables - A variable that originates from outside the system, which you are analyzing which may impact the system under analysis either positively or negatively.

Expedition - Is an artificial or real adventure introduced by a facilitator into the organized brain storming process. The purpose of this exercise is to focus attention away from the goal or problem, gather "data" which seems to have no connection to the task at hand and then make connection between the expedition data and the project.

Exploratory stage - The very beginning stage of organized brainstorming process. The process consists of idea generation techniques designed to generate highly speculative and very playful ideas.

Factor analysis - A statistical method used for to discover a few basic factors, which clarify the connection between variables.

Financial screening - Uses a combination of financial elements to screen ideas. Some examples: initial capital outlay, long-term lifecycle costs, and sales dollar volume by year, risk, cash burn rate, time to break-even.

Free association - used to facilitate access to the unconscious to develop uncensored expression of ideas and impressions.

Horizontal asymptote - A straight line approached by a y-value, curve, as the curve approaches infinity but never quite reaches the line.

Human capital - It is the set of capabilities an individual has, such as knowledge and skills that enables an individual to perform labor that produces economic value.

In-depth interviews - These interviews are used to understand what motivates consumer behavior. This kind of interview is similar to the client interview done by a clinical psychologist.

Key activities - These are the activities that produce the value proposition. Problem solving of all types are included in this component, including the manufacture of a product that has both good quality and sufficient quantities to achieve revenue goals.

Key partnerships - Activities and resource, which are created outside your organization that make it possible to deliver on the firm's value proposition.

Key processes - The means by which a firm delivers value to their customer.

Key resources - These assets are required to deliver on the value proposition. Examples include: physical facilities, vehicles, machines, distribution channels, intellectual property, brands, patents, copyrights, strategic alliances, data, human knowledge and skills, finances, and lines of credit.

KolbeA™ Index - This index measures what you will do or will not do. Intelligence Quotients (IQ) tests tell you what you can do. Personality tests show what you want to do.

Left-brain - some consider this portion of the brain to be more logical, analytical and objective.

Linked Association - Used to facilitate access to the unconscious by using a chain of uncensored expressions in linear order.

Market Attractiveness - Combines and analysis tactical elements, strategic elements and business elements, to determine if (a) market(s) are worth pursuing.

Market concept statement - An expanded version of a concept statement adding such elements as; tangible offering, augmented offering and target segments

Marketing channel - Performs the process of moving goods and services to customers.

Megatrend - A major movement in patterns, which will have an impact on the kind of products and services, which will be purchased in the future.

Metaphor - A figure of speech that describes a subject by asserting it is, on some point of comparison, the same as another otherwise unrelated object.

Mindmapping - A visual organized method of creating, finding, developing and recording different directions.

Multidimensional scaling - Used in marketing for analyzing the preferences and perceptions of respondents, the output from multidimensional scaling is placed on a visual grid known as a perceptional map.

Myers-Briggs Type Indicator (MBTI) - Measures psychological preferences in how people perceive the world and was developed from the work of C.G. Jung.

Opportunity assessment - Focuses on the ability to identify the zone of opportunity which is where external market intersects with competitive trends and a business's ability to deliver a product or service.

Organized brainstorming - A free-flowing creative process within a structure to accomplish a given task.

Power of two - The theory that it takes two people with complementary skills and abilities to help maximize performance. An example maybe an operations-minded person with a marketing minded person.

Preliminary market concepts - A concise, initial description of the product or service.

PRIZM® - Nielsen PRIZM is a set of geo-demographic segments for the United States. PRIZM is used for customer segmentation identification.

Profit formula - The economic plan that outlines how a company will create value.

Project statement - The statement should present an innovation objective broadly in one short sentence and supported by the desired project parameters.

Promising opportunity - Defined as an intersection between a trend and one's ability (strengths) to deliver what a customer needs, wants and desires.

Proto-ideas - Beginning or incomplete ideas.

Prototypes - A working model of the final product or service.

Qualitative research - Research designed primarily to explore and understand customer activity and feelings to help clarify the concept(s).

Quantitative research - Research designed primarily to explore and understand customer activity and feelings to help clarify the concept(s).

R&D - A commonly used abbreviation for research and development; used most often to refer to the development of new products and services

Regression analysis - A statistical process to help obtain a functional relationship between variables.

Respondent group - A group of people who match the target market of a product or service are brought together for the purpose of understanding the groups perceptions, opinions, beliefs and attitudes about the product or service.

Revenue streams - Methods by which money comes into a company. Examples of revenue streams are product sales, usage or subscription fees, licensing or rental agreements or the charging of brokerage, real estate or consulting fees and/or advertising fees.

Right brain - considered by some to be more intuitive thoughtful subjective and deals with metaphors, dreams, humor, intuition and ambiguity. Fantasies, paradoxes, hunches and generalizations play out here.

Sales force and technical studies - The process of analyzing sales reports, personal observations, customer letters, emails, conversations with customers, and customer surveys.

Screening - Is the process of identifying the requirements, such as regulations, and success factors necessary to successfully address in order successfully launch and market products and services.

Segment trends - Is a flow which is found in a portion of the population.

Storyboard - A technique of combining pictures and text to bring a concept into focus so it can be tested and refined.

Strategic screen - Some examples of strategic screening elements are; core competencies, long term growth potential, fit with current customer's compatibility with sales force, improvement in quality.

Tactical screen - Some examples of tactical screens include degrees of competition, ability to deliver product or service, ability to support product, availability of supplier vendor options, ability to distribute product, ability to provide R&D.

Tangible offering - Turns the core offering or benefit into a basic product which customers would purchase.

Target segments - A set of buyers with similar wants, purchasing power, geographical locations, buying attitudes and buying practices.

User attitude studies - These studies gather information on individuals to see how they structure their perception of reality and how that perception influences their response to that reality.

Value proposition - Refer to how well products or services meet customer needs or solve customer problems.

Visualization - Uses imagination to visualize something that might be or could be, including products and services.

About the author

Daniel Tepke worked for several years as associate dean for management and budget at the University of Chicago Booth School of Management. During this time he honed his thinking about the processes and tools necessary to develop successful products and services as well as how to create and run a successful business.

Currently, Tepke serves as the president of Satori Inc., a company focused on executive coaching and group process facilitation to catalyze extraordinary cooperative experiences. This company offers a multistep process to provide participants with insights, information and custom tools to solve business problems. Assignments include strategic planning, new product development and annual plan reviews, including projects of all types from most industry groups, ranging from high tech to higher education.

Prior to Satori, he served as senior vice president of North Park University in Chicago, where his teams used some of the techniques found in this book to restructure tuition, reposition the school in the community perception and among potential students, his work increased enrollment by 34.9 percent, increased net revenue by 58.7 percent and substantially improved athletic recruitment.

He also served as the senior vice president and chief operating officer of the Golden Rule Insurance agency, where he employed the techniques and tools found in this book. Of the many teams he coached, many continue to use research methods included here, like one-on-one interviews and focus groups. This team created and successfully implemented small group Medical Savings Accounts, developed training programs for both senior and mid-level managers, and increased interpersonal skills.

His experiences serve as the basis for this book. More information about the author can be found on LinkedIn at http://www.linkedin.com/pub/daniel-tepke/7/81a/230.

Comments from the author

While it is helpful to understand some business concepts, it is by no means a requirement. If this project involves a team, the team should develop clear guidelines regarding task division between its members. The material should provide everyone with a beneficial, effective learning experience.

During my time at the University of Chicago, business schools and universities generally had not ventured into new entrepreneurial business endeavors. As these educational changes took place, the mission of this school was to explore and perform cutting edge research. In the absence of experts available to meet the needs of those who required idea assistance, I began to receive calls, many of which I referred alumni. Some of the alumni to whom I referred calls frequently complained about the large percentage of these ideas; they expressed concern, saying these ideas were not researched thoroughly enough. In fact, many of these ideas either were already in use or the proposed businesses already existed.

However, I really wanted to help these aspiring entrepreneurs. Therefore, I needed a method by which to screen both the concepts and their creators before passing them along to others for review. Long before the existence of the Internet, I often asked a very easy, old-school questions of these would-be entrepreneurs: "Have you bothered to check the *Yellow Pages* – the phone book – to determine if anything like this currently exists?" If the product exists, is your product superior in some important way to the consumer? There are few new to the world products most are revisions and improvements. For many, these two questions were sufficient to force them to rethink their ideas.

As time evolved, I became involved with an innovative class created by former advertising executive Dave Echols and Professor Harry Davis. This class, which became known as the New Products Laboratory, combined experiential learning with real-world problem solving. This method involved a real client or team performing a real task in real time. Highly motivated MBA students performed tasks using domain-specific knowledge supplied by the corporate team, along with theoretical knowledge supplied by students and faculty members who coached them through the process. Each student and team coach served a very important function.

During my time with this lab, I helped develop this "coach" role, along with a number of tools and processes to help them develop their business ideas and concepts. I also became one of these coaches. My lab experiences helped formalize what I had been doing all along in a couple of ways. It helped formalize a systematic approach for solidifying a business idea and also formalized a method for how to coach individuals and teams along the process.

This coaching may involve how to run an organization, work with a team or help an individual. As I developed this book's structure, I wanted the book serve as the coach, to have it ask questions, as well as provide examples and practice exercises. Each person or team must find the right coach who appropriately meets their needs. An effective coach possesses many of following attributes. The coach:

- Puts your interests first

- Is easy to work with

- Is approachable

- Can make the work fun

- Has extensive experience, which is both broad and deep

- Offers great ideas and alternatives

- Keeps you focused on the ideas and alternatives at hand

- Keeps you focused on both tasks and goals

- Provides reality checks

- Maintains a Socratic approach. This approach is a technique that asks a series of questions rather than provide information. It is the student's task to answer the questions. By doing so, the student gains knowledge.

- Makes sure you do not tackle more than can be handled

- Ensures sufficient practice and research time are allotted

- Pays attention to details

- Asks questions that stimulate and cause you to be explicit and deliberate when you take actions

- Suggests outside resources and offers theoretical knowledge that proves helpful to your thinking to solve the tasks at hand

- Is available and supportive

- Allows you to work through tough situations

- Allows mistakes and helps you learn from these mistakes.

- Provides feedback

A coach should not:

- Make the task at hand their own, but allows the task to remain yours

- Make it all about the coach rather than being focused on you and your project

Having shared some of my background and how a common thread involving new initiative work runs through my career, I believe my experience – and this book – can also assist you in hatching your business idea.

5

www.ingramcontent.com/pod-product-compliance
Lightning Source LLC
Chambersburg PA
CBHW060006210326
41520CB00009B/841